The Treasures of
Divine Love

AWAKENING YOUR
SOUL PURPOSE

by
LANCE HARRINGTON

ISBN-13: 978-1539822899
ISBN-10: 1539822893

Cover Design by Gaelyn Larrick Copyright 2016.
www.gaelynlarrick.com

Thanks to Artist Paul Heussenstamm for contributing artwork
of mandalas, etc., for this book. As per Copyright laws, no use of
this book's artwork is permitted to be reproduced without express
permission of the Artist and/or the Author.

Thank you to Jessica Vineyard of Red Letter Editing
(www.redletterediting.com) for editing this work
and to Jeff Altemus of Align Visual Arts
(www.alignarts.com) for the book interior.

Also, thank you to Catalina Van Haayen for her
photography on the back cover design.

Printed in the United States of America.

Seek the Divine
and you will realize that you are already
universally rich,

For the seeds of Spirit
are the investments of God.

Our Journey

One of the biggest things to know as human beings,
is to realize we are loved so much more than it
may seem sometimes,
and to know the Universe loves us more than we can imagine.

Feeling, remembering,
and comprehending the Universe's love
is why we are here.

Light Vision

Imagine light around all those you see throughout the day.
God and the Angels light bouncing off the souls of the earth.
This will bring an expanded state to your whole being.
There are always reminders to boost us closer to God.

Dedicated to

I dedicate this book to my family.
I also dedicate this to Win, Thai Buddhist Master,
and Helen.

With love, respect, and appreciation.

The accumulation of positive love and spirit granted me all
the love to share with all peoples, yes... but my Mom instilled
within me the love to always be good, loving and sweet.

So lots of credit and acknowledgement must go to her for who
I am and what I become. Her love is deep within my heart.

Acknowledgments

Thank you to my family; you are the sunshine on my angel's wings. Thank you for your warm, pure, and bright golden love. I am deeply grateful for you. Thank you so much for loving me and teaching me to always see the beauty in all of life. Thank you to all my friends for always being there with your hearts wide open.

To Master Win for your love and care; your beautiful heart reflection and spiritual discipline lit more flames of love within me, inspiring me and sprouting little seeds that were already within me, to be a healthier, happier, and more compassionate, loving being for all beings. You openly lived and shared the benefits of having a meaningful and highly fulfilling spiritual practice, and you helped give me a taste of that joy.

Helen, thank you so much. You truly saved my life and inspired me to live, and to always stay positive.

Thank you to Paramahansa Yogananda (and all the great masters). I loved reading *Autobiography of a Yogi* and his extensive library of chants, music, and profound talks and teachings for the world. I've also enjoyed the wonderful book The Urantia Book and the books written by His Holiness The Dalai Lama, Thich Nhat Hanh, and Reverend Michael Beckwith.

Contents

Introduction

This book, *The Treasures of Divine Love*, is a treasure to me. After writing my first book, *The Undercover Yogi*, I didn't think I was going to be able to write any more. I felt that I wrote and expressed all I could for myself, God, and the world. I thought to myself, "what else is there to express, and how will I be able to give more than the first book?" I kept meditating daily, and writings kept coming in. My intention was to go deep within in silent sitting meditation, to heal my mind, give my body more energy, and remain in gratitude for existing—humbled by life and its great mystery—remembering God and the Universe's love, and to send good energy to the Earth, myself, and all beings. This left me with the thoughts, "How will I give to the world more writings, more inspiration, more of my energy and love? How can I give the raw, juicy energy that is dripping from life, and express The Treasures of Divine Love?" In that moment, a bell went off in my head and my heart, and the name of this new book was born.

I hope this book *Treasures of Divine Love* will bring inspiration to all who peruse its pages. We all need inspiration; we all need love. We all need and enjoy positive energy. At times while I pondered this book, I thought maybe I will just keep it all to myself. I thought that I would just keep reading it in secret, pondering more and more about God, the Universe, and the presence of love spread out all over the world. This thought was very fulfilling and so romantic for me.

But then I thought, "How could I keep it all to myself? I must share it!"

When we tap into some magic, we don't always have to let it all out right away.

We can let it simmer, right up until keeping it to ourselves becomes impossible, and if it's that magical, then maybe show others in secret. And then share it with the world!

I hope you enjoy *The Treasures of Divine Love*. May you find what you are looking for.

Thank you, Creator Mother and Father for all of life, thank you for our existence. We remain open to love and are in awe under your special and watchful care.

*An intention, a remembrance, and a vision for our soul's
deep journey into eternity's arms.*

Wishing for Your Highest & Best

I want your soul to rise, shine, and magnify with every cellular
constructed beam of angelic light, of all the molecular design. I want
your highest and deepest best. I want you to meld your heart so deep
in Spirit that you leave its essence on the Earth for all beings to come. I
want the light of pure love to settle so deep within you that the world,
the whole galaxy, may glow within you. I want the essence of love and
the essential particles of your Earth-body to know, in human form,
the truest meaning of golden, Divine Love. I want all souls to see you
and embrace your every cell in light and love. I want the auric waves
of pure value molecules to dance with your every move throughout
eternity. I want the drops of magic and stardust to wisp in light and
trail behind you wherever you fly. I want your soul to find this true
fulfillment, real potency of self-love with such magnificent description
beyond thoughts or words. May you break the barriers of your deepest
soul desire and go beyond, clear to the Maker, the Beholder, and the
Creator of all. May you see, know, and share its wonders of love with
the world. May you stand and float at the brink of time, ready for your
departure in full fulfillment with the real knowing of God's love.

May you find what you are looking for with an open heart, and may
you let the Spirit keep finding you.

A Simple Prayer Intention

Universal Father & Mother

Universal Father and Mother thank you for all life.

May I be able to express, in my possible error, a message to the souls in the world of at least one drop of your perfection that will equate to, and may I be surpassingly accurate of who and what you are with the sounds or writings that come from my lips or my pen.

God, forgive me for ever trying to express the fullness of your love with words, for there are no words that can be produced to fully reveal your absolute and most superb, mind-shattering, and divinely magnificent Universe and all the grandeur of your gloriously incomprehensible elegance and divine mastery, within your very own mastery. Forgive any error in my mind or in the books as I write them, if they come up short to express your magnificence perfectly to all the perfectly imperfect creatures of this realm or to the angelically perfect beings of this realm.

May I learn to walk gently on your Earth soil, as gently as your angelic spirits can fly in through the atmosphere in space, appear, and still not be seen.

May I give my life fully to your trust and the trust that the Angels have in you, with all your love, and embrace it all within every cell of my being.

May all mortals see your beauty. May all beings wipe their tears away to see and feel your love. For even flowing tears cannot express the supreme gratitude in the heart that is felt by your love. May your love be felt by all beings on this planet, always. May these pages touch the hearts and break open all barriers of mind, barriers that the mind can create sometimes— unknowingly—causing feelings of confusion that we feel closed off from your true and Divine Spirit. It is not possible to be closed off from you, for you are everything, everywhere, at all times, omnipresent.

May all beings have strength throughout their short, Earthly lives to open up more to you. Thank you for all the angelic orders that are under your supreme service for this day, this life, my home, my family, friends, animals, and all beings. Thank you for giving me the breath and the life to write this to you with my body, which has been created by you. Eternally grateful and gratified into eternity.

Words are messages

To express the existence of the Divine

In the communication itself

God dwells

All life, all existence, all breath, all the love in the Universe

It's all God's art

Magic Canvas

There is an invisible artist helping us create our very own masterpiece on the canvas of our lives, an artist skilled beyond the comprehensive explanation of thought.

I have only one suggestion for you in the art of your life. Keep your heart open, no matter what! For the love in your heart is the doorway and the key. Stay close with the Master Creator, and let the force of love guide your heart, your life, your art project that is being created. One day, I assure you, you will look back on the canvas of your life in such deep amazement of the mystical and magical wonders of love, beyond your deepest and wildest beliefs.

In life there is no real end.

Only the beginning of the beginning of the beginning.

3-Step Meditation Guide

Have an interactive journey with the author. Use the meditation guide to start your practice, and write your own thoughts, quotes, and affirmations at the back of the book.

1. Sit on comfortable meditation pillows or sit in a chair.

2. Focuse on the breath. Inhale then on the exhale count 1. Inhale then exhale count 2. Go all the way up to 10. (If you lose track or think about something just start over.)

3. Set a timer from 5 minutes to a whole hour and start your practice.

— MORE INFORMATION —

At some point in your practice as time goes on you will feel more relaxed or even blissed out. Your getting in the zone and after some time you may not want to count anymore! So you can just focus on each breath coming in and out your nose. Enjoy that breath and inner silence.

This will re-energize the whole body and where you will find more of yourself.

An Extra Comfort Technique

If you are needing more emotional support from yourself and want to add more while you do these practices, on your inhale and exhale, to yourself you can say things like, I am loved. The Universe wants the best for me. I am surrounded by golden light. God loves me.

Visualization Technique

If you feel Inspired before your meditations to do some visualization techniques you can send light to yourself, imagining golden light wrapped all around you, send light to your friends, your family, the animal's and all beings on the planet. You can even imagine the ones you love holding you. Or the Angels and God holding you.

To simplify "this" visualization compassion exercise you can just imagine you are looking at the earth from space and send love and light to the whole planet.

Daily Writing Technique

Before you leave your home you can write down on a piece of paper, your goals and what you want to see in your life.

> EXAMPLES:
>
> I want to see myself go to college.
>
> I want to see myself happy and feeling good.
>
> I want to see myself full of love. Treating others well and vibrating a vibration of love.

Then you can put your papers of what you wrote into a special place to you, under a crystal or something letting your intentions charge. Then after a week you could put them in the fire place or something releasing it to the Universe!

Wishing you all lots of love, learning, wisdom and happiness!

Daily Healing Affirmations

The daily healing affirmations to come are very beneficial to say to one self. Feeling deeply within our heart with our intention of the good, and to humble ourselves, expands our love ever more, bringing us deep fulfilment.

We receive these positive healing vibrations in our heart, automatically manifesting more love and abundance in our own life. Forever remembering the love that is so deep within the Universe. Our deep realizations never fail to open up our heart allowing more love in.

Here are some healing affirmations created specifically for you, to embrace more and more love into your whole being.

Divine Love always,

Blessings always!

Paradise is also and always within you!

Healing Affirmations for the Morning Heart

May my and the Creator's hearts be one, so full of love
in the waves of consciousness and bliss.

Heart Opening

Universe, I offer my heart to you. I humbly bow and hold
my heart up in my hands to you. Please take my heart,
and love it as much as you can. I will do my best to feel
all of your mystical and magical Divine Love always.

Overflowing Love

I am full of abundance. I have everything I need. All of my love flows freely from the overflowing showers of the Universe's never-ending bliss supply. I am fully awake and in the miracle of life, growing and expanding to my highest potential. We are the miracles. God gives me everything I need, seen and unseen. All opportunities are right in front of me with open arms. I am nourished, loved, and blessed. Every cell of my being is made by cosmic God energy, and the powers of light and good are literally at my fingertips. This energy of God-light runs through my whole being, emanating back to the Universe.

I am experiencing the miracle of life and my greatest destiny right now.

You Are the Universe

I am as the walking manifestation of the Universe's making,
here expressing the magnificent love of the Universe just
by simply being. All things before now have been created
throughout the billions of years for me to just be here right
now. The Universe's love is grandly felt within my own heart
and throughout all the vastness of space and by other inhabited
planets. Everything was created with the pure intention of love.
Love is our natural state of being. Love is our design. Love flows
through our veins and is ingrained in our genetics. Our souls
are made of pure light and love. We are a part of and are related
to all the enchanted light beings within the Universe. The
seeded molecular structures that we are made of are a part of
everything in space and were infinitely designed and created
for us just to be here right now. The ones here now who
know this are here reminding others of this miracle.
You are the miracle. Life is a miracle. All is well.

A Vessel of Spirit

I am a servant of God's light, a messenger of peace, and the gold specks of stardust.

I am open to the Universe moving through every cell of my being.
I am open to all the love that has ever been in eternity.
I am open to all the healing I need that is for my best and highest good.

I am open to all the abundance of Divine Love.
I am open to a loving soul partner to be in my life.
I am open to all the financial wealth to fuel my life's purpose and to be in the best position to share even more with others, and to be in the highest quality Divine service within my destiny.
I am open to be a Spirit helper for others' healings to occur.
I am open to receive all the information I need to be a useful tool for the best and highest good to myself, my family, my friends, all beings, and the planet.

I am growing, changing, and expanding in my gratitude for life, and I am fully activated to love with a clear intention and with the highest-quality clarity and insight.

I am an open, powerful presence on the planet for the people of the world. I am standing before all of God's Angels on the planet, in the Universe, throughout all space and infinity, and they are standing with me.

I am open to embrace the silence of my breath and to allot time for all the meditation hours needed to fully expand my heart, my brain, and my body's function. I am open to be fully activated and available for my Divine direction and highest purpose right now. I am loved unconditionally by the Universe and all beings of pure light. Divine Love always.

The Universe Within

The Divine is universally working for my best and highest good always. I am awakening daily, and my heart is always expanding for the good of all and the planet. I keep my heart open not only for myself, but for all beings. The Universe's love is overflowing and is working within me, helping me to realize the magnitude and magnificence of its unconditional Divine Love always, within and without, from below and above. In my natural calm state of being, I feel this sacred, unique, and special miracle of life within my heart, felt so deeply for life itself. Life is unique, beautiful, and Divinely sacred. My soul is made of the love and light of the cosmos. I know that through any challenges or suffering in the physical reality, there is always the great light and love of the Angels all around me. There is great love and healing for all to experience before the Spirit, in the physical body on the planet, transitions through space to the new journey that is pure with joy. My life is full of Divine Love and miracles that are seen and unseen. I know that feeling, remembering, and comprehending the Universe's love is why we are here.

I Give It All

Creator, Universe, Angels, all orders of light beings: I give my love to you. I give my heart to you. I give my strength to you. I give my body to you. I give my wings to you. I give my thoughts to you. I give my light to you, I give my dark to you. I give my soul to you. I give my life to you. I give my gifts to you. I give my talents to you. I give my breath to you. I give my fathers, mothers, sisters, brothers, children, and all my ancestors to you. I give the animals to you, the plants, and the planet to you. I surrender in your light and unconditional, Divine, mystical, magical, magnificent, unsurpassingly — beautiful — Divine — Angelic love beyond thoughts or dreams. You have given freely all of these beautiful things to all of us, and I receive it all fully, and that is why I give, I give, I give, I give it all back to you.

For without you, I would not be.

Daily Healing Affirmation

I want to see what is the best and highest good for
all beings happening throughout the world.

We can say this daily healing affirmation to ourselves
and visualize being in space—as far away as the
moon is—looking back at the Earth.

Sending love and light to the whole planet and all beings.

Wisdom Gems
& Poems

Love is Like a Floating Lotus

Love is like a floating lotus, perfectly preserved within eternity,
forever and ever.

Love Is

Love is the inner experience that your heart feels. Love is like the warmth from the sun and still not fully expressible by nature, but only if seen by the observers of eternity. Love is unchangeable. Paradise is always resting on your fingertips. Love introduces power to the weak and brokenhearted. Love is speechless and still, and still not fully expressible in physical form. Love goes beyond a romantic relationship with another human being. Love transcends space and time, yet still *is* space and time. Love is extendable but unchangeable, and variable with the velocity of light. God's love, even if described with thousands of pages to share the attributes of love, still would be too much to take in fully to the aura or cortex of the brain. Love is simple. Love is simply complex. Love is weightlessly dense. Love is the light that could shadow the whole galaxy by another one. Love exists. Love is. Love goes beyond song, sounds, and melody. Love surpasses beyond thoughts and imagination. Even a newborn baby yearns to just give the love it feels from before birth. Love is beyond birth. So much love will a child give naturally. We all just want to share and deeply express the Spirit of Divine Love. This gift and highest quality and deepest blessing comes from our Angels, the Divine Mother Spirit, and God, who is fusing that unbreakable love to all beings and the still young and evolving human race.

You are love drifting through space, speechlessly in awe.

Drunk on Divine Love

My eardrums hear the vibrations and sounds and feel the hums
and rings of a thousand grounds as the sun sits gracefully, ever
beautifying.

Watching the Earth wisping by, many days still pass tirelessly in
one moment's breath.

Forever my eyelashes grasp God's powers lovingly, landing down
on all the heaven's miracles.

Overjoyed and laughing uncontrollably, observing eternity's
inherent duties, lavishly inhaling the stardust medicine for all.

My mind speedily swept away,
my soul's thirst is eternally satisfied and birthed into this new day,
observing the Divine consciousness for all beings granted
infinitely by the Master's blessing.

Searching and always finding, seeking and always reminding
the hearts of all to take loving refuge in the deep ecstasy of silent
meditation.

So blessed in its unfolding, upholding, unfailing, uniting,
unifying, Angelic, crystallized blanket of galactivated positive
energy.

Evolving, revolving, solving the mysteries and finding all the keys
to open the heart.

Being a part of the Master's grace, seeing the spark of God in
every face, everywhere, every time, in everything.

This ringing bell sets in as all my chakras spin from within,
guiding me on a magical carpet, unconditionally drunk on the
wine of pure love and Spirit expansion with the simple and yet
sublimely incomprehensible Divine.

DING!

Life's Magical Mystery

No need to make things seem more mystical and magical.
They already are!

Drunk on the Golden Divine Nectar

Sitting at the heart's window,
the eternal Divine shines in and bathes me,
gifting my every cell with intuitive, infinite knowledge.

The breeze, like the breath of God;
the golden warmth of the sun, like the blanket of Angels.

The comfort and knowing of the long journeyed destiny deeper
into paradise, like the unbroken love that is blissfully captivating,
evolving, embracing, entrancing, elevating, shocking, gazing,
fixed, transfixed, translucence, transcending, that transpires for
the Divinely paralyzed drunk yogi in the form of a body hosting
the arrival of Angels.

Words have no description of this sacred melting nectar of God
communion.

Drunk on this Divine Love, I must admit.

Sipping of the wine in Divine meditation I sit.

A Spiritual alcoholic I am.

This is what a humble master will feel like
in the fabric of the universal timeless hours of deep meditation.

Divine Romance

Trying to comprehend the vastness of the Universe's love is
like a Divine romance.

Poetry to the Master of Creation

Your energy directs the clouds. Your voice brings on a whisper.

Your heart sounds the Universe's bell to call in an audience of Angels, or the wisdom of a sister.

Your touch slides in vibrating and eminating with a calm relaxing energy, soothing the soul and every cell moistens for the pure oxygen of breath. Every moment is a sacred moment, slow, stimulating, and intentional. All in a moment, in-tune, open, receptive. Heart drenched in galaxies, overturned to a direct connection with God, blanketed in the knowing of this connection in existence. Laughter flying in at the seat of Angels, the chants of all Earth beings heard though the layers of reality intertwined with the seraphic* umbilical cord of love itself. Creation molecules, star dust, opelesence, amber hue, infinity frequencies, and the whole of energy, existing records and insights of Spirit antedating consciousness of mind. Your light is a candle crystal shaped remembrance of eternity and everlasting joy, relaxing peace, deep in compassion and forgiveness.

Full in this heart you are. One by one, swiftly, your waves are always existent, undescribably remarkable, gemming essence pursuing and piercing humanity and creation itself. Your flavor is rich beyond gold, speechless in expressions, and playfully always awake.

You're like a Rumi expression intensified.

The Poetry to the all of all. The love of love. The holy Master and Maker of the Universe.

---

*Seraphic: *adj. Characteristic of or resembling a seraph or seraphim (an Angelic being).*

Taste the Universe

Optimism is like using a telescope to see, expand your own positive awareness, and comprehensively feel and taste the Universe.

The Living Love

Only do what you love.

If you can't always do what you love, then learn to do everything you do *with* love. Then you will succeed, and your purpose will be achieved. Your life is a miracle, and you are awakening every moment to experience that miracle of "you" and of "it."

The time is now, always and forever. The presence of love is expansive, infinite, unbroken, weightless, invisible, visible, imaginative, extraordinary, extremely ultimate, illuminating. The presence of love is powerfully, playfully, prayerfully, peacefully, cheerfully, openly, internally, externally, extensively, distinctly universal. The presence of love is universally, Angelically, breathlessly, ceaselessly, creatively, flawlessly, doubtlessly, effortlessly, impressively, entertainingly, interestingly, increasingly, endearingly, measurably, immensely, chillingly, objectively, intensively, blessedly, necessarily, lovingly, successfully, awesomely, and multidimensionally unconditional.

Your awareness is Divine and intelligent. It is now, and will forever always be, awakened in you for your greatest and highest good in your journey throughout eternity.

Miracles

There are miracles happening every day in our lives.
It is up to us to see and experience them!

God's Beauty and Love

If you were able to hear God's voice or poetry through your tears, you would never forget the taste of the eternal truth and Divine bliss of beauty forever.

For your eyes would shed tears forever in your material, mortal body.

Your body would not be able to fully hold all of the Universe's love.

This love is endless, timeless, limitless, leaving us all speechless. Like a river, your tears would pour and pour, for God's love is infinite and beyond comprehension or imagination.

With your daily meditations, one day, I assure you, with your sincere practice, you will feel this realization truly for yourself.

With each person on this planet meditating and getting to a place within themselves to fully realize this, ahhh . . . then the true beauty begins.

In time we will have a world fully immersed in what is called unity and universal love.

I send love and light to all beings.

May the ocean represent all of the tears from all mortals in the material bodies who have ever lived in Divine union or may have died in the illusion of separateness. We are never truly separate from all things and all beings. May all the water of the world represent all the water that would ever pour out of every mortal's eyes if they were to realize the magnitude and vastness of all the Universe's love.

Opening into Love

The biggest high you will ever get to experience
is from the realization of God's existence.

Meditation & the Golden Flame

As real as the lit flame,
your fuel lights up my golden fire for the Divine;
your energy keeps these molecules existing.

This warmth of Spirit forever burns inside my heart with this golden glow and the reflection of magical healing crystals.

After I bathe myself in silent meditation, I burn your trees of love, a palo santo stick.

I inhale your every scent.

I embrace and watch the hot flames of energy that you create with all your elements.

I see the beginnings of ashes turn into the dusts that transform lives, all souls into a blanket as slippery as silk. O how my heart burns with the romance of your smoke from your love, O how my eyes shine from your sight and the clearness of your healing crystal.

I feel your presence.

Your warmth and smoke touch my skin and linger all around me like your Angels, lifting me up, illuminating my cells in waves of calm, deep reflection, gratitude, and ecstasy.

I know you are forever with me.

With this gift and knowing of your love,
I am forever drunk on Divine Love.

Heaven is also within You

Every day do yoga, eat healthy, and meditate,
and you won't have to look for heaven — it will find you!

The Mystical Magical Land

My heart sits full with peace, like being one with a thousand
honeysuckles. Golden nectar entrapped in every cell of my being
on the best day of my life. Memories, dear memories of the
Universe's voice overshadow and anchor my highest wisdom,
resting on the palace of my love. Levitating wisdom wisps in
and around my auric field, like sitting with all the great Masters.
This experience, and tea — like God's best wine — produced the
mighty Universe and university of Angels. Ahhh, so touched in
the Graceland of inner inheritance of the Spirit of truth, we all
share in the Earth's depths of life and death. It says "Drink me
in and share my fruits to all men and women honoring the land
of the world. Let them also drink of the sacred melting rainbows
showering unconditional bliss and unifying, crystallized love
to all their homes—a reminder of the external sanctuary and
paradise within them, and the magnificent journey toward a true
and real paradise within me."

The Maker

God, you are the maker of reality and the Spirit's gifts and dreams of the stars in the galaxy. Your Presence is the entertainment for our hearts, and it is your love that keeps us all alive.

Spirit's Voice

I am like a blanket of roses sitting on a cool breeze, galactivated by cosmic energy.

I am the Universe moving through space and the light that remains beyond time.

I am the Zen garden at all the peaceful meditation hours.

I am an Angelic body made of Divine Love and light.

I am the Om in the musical of life that is playing on the Universe's CD.

I am the messenger of light and bringer of protection to carry your soul home.

I am the whisper behind all your compassionate, understanding, and empathetic thoughts.

I am the feeling of love within every laugh or tear in the experience of comfort.

I am love.

I have been sent by the Divine Creator.

I am the Spirit.

Love Everywhere

If you are searching for the love in the Universe, just look around.
It is everywhere!

Your Class is My Temple

Your class is my temple; your heart is my sword; your energy is my shield; the valleys of your destination are my home. Your tears are the Angels' gifts, your body is the host, your walk is Divine; my footsteps are a memory of eternity in the now. Your eyes and your lips embrace eternity; your dreams are from the stars; your God is the only real maker and Creator of all names; your existence is precious, and I love you. You are loved beyond your thought-streams or dreams. Incomprehensible is the vast ecstasy the Master provides. Unfolding truth he reveals, the love of lifetrons*. Your bones are like a dream, and your soul is worth all the gems in the whole galaxy. May this love settle in your heart, deeper and deeper, as we watch in awe, emitting the light of God's existence.

*A term utilized by Paramanhansa Yogananda; p14, Vol I, of *Second Coming of Christ: The Resurrection of the Christ Within You*. "These casual ideas emit a magnetic force of light and intelligent energy, which I call *lifetron*, that form the astral body of man."

Devotion to Love Creates its Own Legacy.

 *She Speaks*

With our awareness we move with Gods light.
Waves of the invisible.

The Creator is in control of all uplifting Spirits.

The trees call to us: "Naturally, nature, nurtures."

The wind whispers: "Feel, feel, feel me, the heartbeat of all things animals and beings. Come back home to that awareness. Feel the bright sun bursting energy created to warm all souls."

— Listen

Embracing Love

Imagine and know there are Angels around you
all day and see what happens!

The Power of the Heart

The depth of our hearts will always teach us
what we need to know.

Through the path of our joys and struggles,
our open hearts will be the only thing
remaining and unconditional.

The deep valleys of the heart are beautiful.
Its trees are there to climb,
and lakes are there to swim and surrender into.

The power of the heart is gentle like rain,
soft like cotton,
sweet like strawberries,
and shy as a fox.

The rivers of the heart
follow them through the forest.
Open your wings
and fly your way home
to the oceans of joy.

Water helps all things grow.
It will rain, it will always rain.
O, the tears, they will come,
and they will be your best friends for the rest of your life.

Mystical Being!

O, how do the rains and sun part from the heavens if thou art not
seen by the storms of your eternal beauty and perception ?

The inner flight of your soul is like the coat of love to keep the souls
of the planet warm and eternally embraced. Gratitude drips from thy
heart of waterfalls that ends up at the seat of thy shore.
Oh-so-many will sail in the beauty of your love.

 # *Eternal Freedom*

Lift up your head, let your heart lead.

Passion rises. Your love will feed you,
melting away all your sorrows.

Meditations that follow will give you sight to see the
world's halo, to fill it with all the love and light you want.

Burst your soul free. Be in unity.

Give, craft, and raft in the rivers of eternal freedom
with the real knowing
of the Universe's love
being sent right to your feet.

Set your intention of pure love for all beings and watch your
third eye start seeing Angelic love relaxing every cell of your
being.

Opening Deeply

Open up to the omnipotent omnipresence of love that is always
available within every cell of your being.

Letting More Light In

May any sorrows you have be cleared and washed away by the storms of your own positivity.

Your desire to heal, your openness to love, your gratitude for life, your ability to allow the Spirit to transform you will inevitably burst bright light through any clouds of negativity that were once lingering around you. Love and God flow through you, always. The lessons you learn to strengthen your ability to shower yourself with more self-love, more relaxation and peace, more meditation, more Angelic light, are the special treasures of Divine Love.

*God Created everything and
inspired everything good.*

Spirit Song

The love in my heart is beyond a human desire,

The seeds of my soul are always on fire,

The waves of my passion are always in fashion,

The love for the Earth, to the holyest Mansion.

My destinies here, I just shead a tear, for all of my brothers and sisters in fear.

To settle the game, theres no shame in pain, all of my brothers and sisters the same.

Lift your selves up, to the holy cup, and remember sip love and never give up.

We're making change, planets, re arange, sometimes things seem awkward or even strange.

The Angels have are back, were on the right track, feeling positive, never in lack.

We stack and stack our souls in a line, knowing that with God everythings fine.

We're on the Angelic road, it always unfolds, heaven on Earth let the truth be told.

Feel excited, constantly invited, always let the Spirit guide it.

No unknown, always home, heavens gates is where we roam.

Sipping tea, you and me, feeling jolly, always free.

Stars glissining, heart listening, everythings always new, blissed out people on this creation too.

Feeling the trees, swimming in the seas, praying to Creator on our knees.

Forms of Meditation

Think of God and the Angels, and any of your other great
inspirational teachers of love, whenever you are awake or asleep
and in all that you do in life allowing in that positive, optimistic,
calming, and comforting, energy. That is meditation, too.

It's All Connected

In the beautiful framework of the bigger picture in life, we feel fulfilled to dig deeper and deeper into ourselves in meditation or contemplation to find the ultimate mental freedom. To see and observe things in our lives, mystical and magical, and to rediscover our simple, true happiness. After digging deep, deep down in our hearts and connecting in our silent meditation, we also remember to keep our perceptions looking upward to the trees, sun, moon, and stars to gain an even greater awareness of the eternal possibilities of God's ultimate and unconditional power in the Universe. We remember the infinite possibilities of our Divine souls. With that openness, we experience and find more of God's superbly magnifying, never-ending and satisfying, uninterruptedly justifying Spirit responsiveness, to be speechlessly in awe of the Angels flying, and sublimely dignifying, lovingly gratifying, blissfully and undeniably unifying universal love!

Designed by the Universe to be within every cell of your being.

Heart of Compassion

Where does your heart lie? Beneath the breath and wings of Angels. O, may they guard, guide, direct and protect your every move, your every dance and every groove, giving you the strength and courage of a light worker, a bringer of the great light and love. May the Spirit whispers be heard in your ears from the Angelic orders of the Universe.

Love Always

I sit because I love you. I ride the holy prayers of love to the sounds of magical meditation bells and Angels' wings, whistling by a path full of smiling faces, loving hearts, stardust molecules of eternity, sprinkled on the layers of Angelic perception in the movie of our love.

Pure cosmic devotion.

Gifting water, refreshing to the dry desert face of our skin,

in one moment observing the years of human evolution and the Universe's whole of eternity.

For all the years that have ever been. For all the years yet to come.

So much love, so many smiles have poured out in front of all the Universe to see.

The teardrops, the golden nectar of our love, where empathy, hope, and joy twirl as one, uniting each soul as mortal brothers and sisters.

The tears of all representing the Angels' soft whispers of hope for the planet's beating heart.

The survival of the soul.

The rays of light.

O, so many tears on the planet that have been cried

in the journey to find and feel love.

In the journey to find God

—Within

Soul Play

We are forever experiencing depth of the heart
and the miracles in the mystery.

Humble Seeker

You're a dream, a beam, a light, love's wings guided by Angels, a speck of God dust, a miracle beyond time, a Spirit full of energy, empathy, compassion and love, a daughter or a son of the most high, a giver beyond your years, your tears, or the cheers of your peers, your soul sails within eternity in the heaven of all creation, you're a teacher and a watchful and humble seeker, a student to the Divine mother and father of all but still the messenger of the eternal home, your body made of value molecules and your heart of gold, a precious one to all.

The Divine Spirit

Flow like the river
With the Spirit as your sail,
Give all your love to the Universe
And you will never fail.

Yogi Physics

What I mean by the Universe, I am saying that the energy and love summed up by the magnificence of God's creation, times the Angelic realms of the cosmos, times the perfection in the making, times all life in the Universe from molecules and atoms, to all beings existing in all the creation of inhabited galaxies. Equals out to the $E=mc^2$ of all that is. The Everlasting Magnificent Creation squared up to the All that is powerfully and playfully of light and love unconditionally surpassing thoughts, places, and things brings us to even more love.

Overflowing God in all capacity.

Boundless love, Ultimate Wisdom.

Supreme in Compassion.

So we are truly blessed.

The all that is, that is thoughtfully, powerfully and playfully working within all our lives is of beautifully omnipresent and of omnipotent nature and is upholding and theoretically holding all of the realities of all the realities together. Let me say that again: is upholding and theoretically holding all of the realities of all the realities together. Is holding all of the Universe together, perfectly.

Essentially.

Grateful, loved, blessed, nurtured, nourished, received, honored, and so humbled by love.

Mystical Poet

To God, Universe, and Angels of love:
you are the true mystical poets. I am in awe,
and I am forever just an observer of your existence.

For Love I Rise

I fall in love with love itself,

melt in its beauty, shower in its ice, thankful in the reflection,
blown away by its presence, vulnerable in its wake, infused with
its magnificence, humbled at the door,

beyond speechless in its perfection.

Consciousness is in us all and is awakening us exponentially.

Inner Treasures

He or she who reaches for God's love, and finds it deep within their own heart, experiences profound things. These experiences may include the following and more: miracles, healings, the whispers of eternity, the meditation path, an abundance of love, an opened mind and an expansion of the heart, value molecules, the Angels' poetry, the art plasma of creation, the isle of paradise, optimistic realities, the one behind the projector screen, colors within black and white, clarity through any judgments, a language of love, all about family, gratitude, Spirit creation and ceremony, the intelligence in the elephants and dolphins, sacred geometry in visions, the sun and moon's unconditional love, a home where ever you are, fairies, light beings, devas of the Earth, compassion spread out all over the world, heavenly music, a festival full of yogis, the stories of creation.

Morning Love

Morning love drops enhance your Spirit molecules, illuminating
your heart opening, your soul ceremony, in everything that you are,
surrounding you in the cosmic rays of Divine Love and light.

The New Beginnings

When I eat, I am grateful.

When I eat, I think of all those who are hungry in the world.

When I drink, I think of all those who are thirsty.

When I breathe, I think of all those who don't have clean air.

When I bathe, I allow my body to relax in gratitude, bathing in the deep healing and fully aware of the gravitational experience my body feels day in and day out.

When I am in silence and choose to go days in silence, I think of and visualize a world where, on some days, the whole planet and all its people just sit in silence, quietly and calmly in meditation together, having the deep inward self-realization that we are all in this together.

When I cry, I think of all the people throughout human evolution who have had broken hearts.

When I laugh, I remember when a laugh reminded me to just live one more day.

When I speak, I think of all those who didn't get to or who don't have a voice.

When I hear, I think of all those who are deaf and have never even heard the sounds of their own parents' voices.

When I run, I think of all those who don't have the ability to even walk.

When I smile, I think of all those who don't feel beautiful.

Before I sleep, I think of all those who have insomnia or are too cold at night to rest.

When I love, I think of all those who fought, lived, and died trying to.

When I meditate or pray, I think of all those who have been too confused to connect back to Spirit, who are too busy to be grateful, too self-absorbed in ego to truly be humble and give respect to dear life.

When I break, my heart shatters and pain fills my whole body, my heart, my chest, my brain. The tears stream, pour and pour, and my veins pulsate, and my whole being is empty, not knowing what lies before me in this life. Once again, I bow and am again intensely and understandably humble before the Earth.

And then I remember to bend, for there is no end.

Only the beginning of the beginning of the beginning.

Earth Family

We are all brothers and sisters,
we are all brothers and sisters,
we are all brothers and sisters.
We are all related!
Indeed!

Inner Peace Lasts Forever

Happiness is circumstantial. Inner peace is forever. Pain, sorrow, joy, beauty, and love are all things experienced in life.

Depending on circumstances, your happiness may sway this way or that way, but one who feels good with who they are—with the knowing of the Spirit, God, the Angels—have a true inner peace that will last forever.

You may not always be in a seemingly happy-feeling circumstance, but being content in your heart of hearts, with a trust of the Universe, and with an expanding, grateful heart in this gravitational experience, is worth a thousand lifetimes.

You Can Always
Find Your Happiness
in Deep Gratitude.

With Love

I want to honor all those who do yoga to strengthen themselves. I want to honor all those who eat well and exercise to feel better in their lives. I want to honor all those who do silent sitting meditation and go deep into their hearts. I want to honor all the ones who can't walk or exercise because they can't move their own bodies, can't hear or even speak. I want to honor all those who, even if they can't move, try to have positive thoughts for themselves and the world as a practice of sending love and light to all beings. I want to honor all those who are not in the place yet to think or do good for themselves or others. We all are here in our experience of life on this planet. May we all live in peace and come out of any obstacles with improvement and betterment in the learning for self-love and deep love for the Earth and all beings.

Every Day's Quote

Every individual in the world
could have their very own
"who could be more grateful" contest
and change the world.

Mother Earth's Beauty & Love

Morning meditations bring our hearts into full sensation,
for when we kiss each other we charge like electricity,
enough to power a whole city.

I know we should only worship the Divine Mother and Divine
Father, creators of all life in the Universe.
But when I see your beauty, Earthly Mother,
I feel my knees shaking, wanting to fall and kneel to your feet.

I hope my fall wakes up those still not yet awake,
for you give life to so many.

I hope all may see and respect your beauty.

Supreme potential

Imagine your family and loved ones holding a clear Crystal, sitting deep in meditation, while communing deep within their heart and God. See them in their highest potential with Supreme compassion and love.

Gratitude in the soul of the Earth

I am no saint. I like to paint. I never had to faint. I always
see blues, purples, yellows, pinks, greens, oranges, and reds,
white beds, strands of lotus flowers, smoke rings on the clouds
of eternity, honey and bears, people, kind hearts, elephants,
gratitude in a straw, life in a cow, joy in a bucket of rose petals,
freedom on wings, love in essence, grace caterpillers, expression,
full of expressions, blending beauty, beyond humility. Life
changer, wow! blessings, the adventure, look, see? touch, blend
gifts, reasoning, deep realization, ahhhhh, so much love.

Divine Limitlessness

I have no age.
The love within my heart will live on forever.

To See or Not to See?

That is the answer to a lifelong question.

Today is but a dream.
Tomorrow is full of light.

My heart sings to a reflection
of the stars in the night.

Yesterday the Divine blessed me
with a flame of delight,

guiding my way home
with a torch blazing bright,
glowing like a core
of galactivated, loving, Spiritual insight.

Settling in my heart,
life's mystery speaks a gentle sound.
I heard all the souls, flickering, walking on the ground.

As a portal door opens,
my cellular structure changes
as I walk through the galactic center
humbled by all the great sages.

A calm, soothing voice
echoes softly, and enters into my ears

until I hear all the joys,
all the cheers,
all the tears
of all the souls,
of all the Earth's many years.

As the Angelic helpers instantaneously
swept me up in all the heaven's warm blankets,

they quickly blinked,
illuminating my weightless body and lifting it
effortlessly.

I begin weeping
for all of our mortal, gravitational sorrows.

This bestowed blessing
is so I may hear all the souls' callings
for all the Creator's blessings
asked for ceaselessly,
throughout all the galactic realm of Spirit circuitry,
in all the many different ways possible.

My heart knows, in this single moment,
that it is through our daily meditations on Earth
that we envelope a greater connection to our hearts
and the Divine Creator of all,
giving us a true fulfillment
of the true knowing
that the Divine is always with us.

We shall stay disciplined to our daily meditations
and remain clear in our heart of hearts
because we remember that when we seek the Divine
Creator Mother and Father in the depths of our hearts
and souls, the magical, mystical synchronizations seem
to just begin to start for us.

We begin to sail blissfully closer to eternity in the deep,
Divine ecstasy of our own hearts.

The heart's potential is way more than most of us may
ever know, and yet we all know a little more about it
each day.

May we flow forward on our Spirit journey to supreme oneness with all things, remembering that this body is temporary, and we will inevitably fly free, closer to the great source of all things.

When the mind is still and calm, truth enters the ears clearly, like music echoing through a tunnel. Love is all there is and all that is of value.

When the mind gains more awareness from the heart and understands deeper into the illusions of desire in the material world, we begin to know more about an eternal love.

Let us commune with this one moment's breath together as if it were our last breath:

I love myself, my family, my friends, the animals, and all beings.

You have all shown me so much love and have been a part of so much of my life and the experiences of what life is on this planet, and helped teach me of what I love so dearly!

Aho!*

---

*In some Native American tribes, *aho* is often used as a greeting or to end a prayer (similar to the use of "amen"). It is often accompanied by "Mitakuye Oyasin."

Tears and joys are the Angels' whispers throughout the ethers of time.

444

44444444444444

Sailing Deeply

Call me the castaway if you wish,
who is sailing deeply within,
deep into the unknown for all beings,
riding the waves of meditation

and sailing deeply into the cosmic ocean
of my own heart
with a ship full of the best wine,
beauty, goodness, and truth.
Forever free and so drunk on Divine Love.

I do what I can for God, the Angels, and the world.

Spirit Heals All

We are all healing in so many ways. Everyday, I drop my attention into my heart and even cry if I need to, asking God to open and expand my heart even more. I ask that any emotions or feelings that may be keeping me from being in an ultimate state of peace to please be removed. I say to God, "God, please use me for the highest good of all. Open my heart up so I may let Spirit flow through me. O Spirit, I know you speak through the technicolored auric circle I see under my eyelids in the long deep relaxing hours of meditation. I feel and see your wisdom lingering within me and resting right at my fingertips." I feel the weight and the sorrows of the world lifted off me. "When I pull myself into nature and into the deepness of your silent sitting meditation and prayer, I sense and know your Angels are here with me and all of us. I imagine, feel, and know You are here with me. I also know all the masters and helpers of your pure light are here as well. Nothing is ever lost, for you are everywhere, in everything, and all things and beings go back to you. We all will be with You for all of time. Give this heart the openness and blossoming of a lotus, and to flow like the rivers. Thank you for giving me peace, and peace to all who wish to swim in your joy."

Waves of Love

Sending you deep waves of light consciousness and bliss. All love is full within you. You are a great soul, and you are showing your love and calm being with a bounty of humility and natural compassion for the world. You are a supreme being of God, a helper of good.

Good Rain

Those who are big thinkers eventually learn to not think,
but to feel the love deep within their hearts.

Where most men's hearts may fall cold and dormant, far away
from Spirit, the Yogi sits and wears his heart on his sleeve.

He then gets up and does a rain dance
to call down the Angels
to drench all people with Divine Love.

Awareness always seems to be the key that turns the world into a better place.

The Destiny of the Heart

Truly, the magic of life is within you, within the heart, and within the Spirit cortex of the brain. With lots of meditation, one is internally satisfied by the soul in a special way. It is developed through time, building more and more clarity, a confidence, an inner strength, an independence of self, an unbreakable trust with the Universe, a wealth of inner wisdom lingering within your very own heart and at your fingertips, a calm soothing relaxation, and the ability to grow more in that love, living more abundantly and seeing more in an Angelic way. Through time, the heart and mind settle together, listening more to that place of the soul knowing and the higher self. The goal is to become closer to the source of love within your own heart and feel the Spirit of your own Divine soul.

The Masters will be waiting there, the Angels too, and I will also be waiting, and many others!

The Universe will be waiting, God will be waiting. The world is waiting for you!

Hour-long meditations are like having a sip of tea with God.

Days of Gratitude

Today I fell in love, yesterday I fell asleep, tomorrow when I wake up, I hope to hear my heart beat. I hope to fall deeper in love and into my meditations, to once again fall in love with love itself.

Until All Are Fulfilled

My heart is full with love and Divinely fulfilled by the existence
of God. Not until each human being is full with Divine Love and
the world is in superconsciousness and at peace will my desires
be completed. May all beings rest in the same blanket of love
knowing that we are here to share it together.

Spirit's Existence

In life, there are only a few things that are for sure and are true and consistent. Spirit's existence, and all else is unknown. So all is well! Get used to your inner lighthouse! Keep your heart consistently open as best you can. Be in gratitude for what you have, and see your life as a miracle! That, in and of itself, will bring more positive light to your whole being, and as you begin to watch more miracles unfold in front of you, you begin to wake up! Wake up to the overflowing, never-ending bliss supply that is full of the goodness of your own perception, the Universe's rivers of abundant peace, and the stimulating, powerful openness to your expanding consciousness. This will consistently bring you in awe of the love and light all around you, magnetizing more and more positivity, love, and light to your optimistic reality, in your all-is-well vibrations, and building that energy and clarity more and more in your meditations, knowing that you are now, and always have been, an important and empowered being on the planet, to share your gifts and help others share theirs. Before, you were just in time lags for short moments and just had to fully wake up! An expanding heart brings expanding good. Here's an affirmation to soak it all in:

I am full of abundance. I have everything I need. All of my love flows freely from the overflowing showers of the Universe's never-ending bliss supply. I am fully awake and in the miracle of life, growing and expanding to my highest potential. We are the miracles. God gives me everything I need, seen and unseen. All opportunities are right in front of me with open arms. I am nourished, loved, and blessed. Every cell of my being is made by cosmic God energy, and the powers of light and good are literally at my fingertips. This energy of God-light runs through my whole being, emanating back to the Universe.

I am experiencing the miracle of life and my greatest destiny right now.

Relaxing into Prayer

We can meditate many hours, have positive affirmations, and do healthy good things for the mind and body. Sometimes we also need to pray. Praying to the Creator has its own benefits and rewards. Humbling down, settling in a deep place of surrender to know and feel that God is truly in control of everything. Instilling in our own mind good prayers for ourselves, others, and the world. What peace will come from this. What peace will be milled from this.
You will feel this peace when you pray.

 *It Is Simple*

 The Stairway to Heaven is

 The Doorway to Love

 Love is the Doorway and the Key

Love So Sacred

Let us always remember to treat everything sacred,
for our Angels are always here with us.
And if we sometimes forget,
may we always remember to not forget.

In the Name of Love

You will find your truth and more truth will come.

Your truth, your reality, your experience, is an individual thing and is unique. You are unique.

My truth is Love. Love, for me, is the ultimate. Love is all we see made by the essence of Love. Love is my master, Love is my maker and my creator of all the dreams of reality; Love created my all-that-is. The God of all names is Love.

What name you give your love is up to you, and you will have your own experience on what name you love to give to your love.

Your teacher of love could be fascinating, brilliant, majestic, mystical, exceptionally genuine, full of the highest good, and is, or was, a bright golden light in the world, made by the very light and love of Love.

Love is the holy name of God.

God is the holy name of Love.

Love is the breath that comes from life for you to speak your words of love.

Everyone can call God or love any names they will, as they will, to define the feelings of love that they get deep within their hearts, about their own lives and loves.

In the end, Love is love.

God is love.

Life is love.

Breath is love.

You are made by love.

You live in love.

You rest in love.

You love in love.

Even through deep pain, you can love and feel love.

Love will hold you.

You can be held by it.

You can love yourself more.

You can find more love within.

You can love the world more by expanding your love within.

You can always learn to love more.

You can experience love always.

Love is how you exist.

Love is the only thing that matters in life.

Love is the answer.

How do you show, express, and expand your love for Love?

How does your love serve you?

What can you do differently to expand or express your love for the highest good for yourself and all?

Loving Others

Love others deeply,
even beyond their perceptions.

The Arrow of Compassion

When our hearts are fully open, we can still be discerning about how and who we choose to share time with. Strong in where we stand and what our balance points are, we live in deep gratitude for the simple things in life, gaining deeper and deeper respect for ourselves, always.

Living in a good way. Allowing love to keep expanding our hearts ever greater, clearing ourselves and opening up, even after seeing and knowing the beatings of the world.

The rollercoaster of moods no longer controls us. We see where truth is and what sustains us.

We learn to cleanse,
Meditate,
Pray,
Stretch,
Surrender,
Allow,
Trust, and
Push on.

From deep within our hearts we walk in this world. It is a double-edged sword.

When you are sharp, you have to learn to be sharper! Stay open and learn the deeper wisdom, more and more, for your highest good: it is a relaxed and, at the same time, a very focused procedure.

It is like meditation; with the practice of meditation, we are pushing ourselves on the fast track faster to end our suffering. Very relaxed and very focused and devoted to expanding our love. Big lessons are on this river toward Divine Love within.

Once we master it, we are ninjas of light, the night of Divine
Love, the arrow of compassion, the crystal ball, the mystical
wizard, an advanced yogi with a degree in love, a statue of wings,
Tinkerbell's fairy dust, the echo from the sounds of OM, the
magnifying glass over our own eye, the watching spy of our
own perception, the author of our new life story, the applauding
audience for our own awards, our own best friend, the scientist
of our own heart, the Angels' helper, the energy of light's great
outlet, the eye of the storm, the peace sign in a war, the healing,
green-colored moss on a tree, the element that exists between
worlds, the flute maker who plays with Kokopelli, the amazing
magical Universe looking back at itself . . .

The stories of the Universe are in the molecules of an atom and on the backs of Angels' wings.

 *Spirit U All*

Spirit is all. Spirit is in everything that makes up the atoms and lifetrons of expanding experience and existence itself. The energy of creation is Spirit.

Behind the curtain of what is seen to the eye is the eye of perception; beyond that is pure love and the Universe glimmering within the sparkles of your eyelids, the light, the energy, the specks of stardust. Spirit particles make up the dreams of reality. This is God's movie.

Everything you do in your life is Spirit u all, and expressing that Spirit is all without you even realizing it. Of course, the Divine Spirit indeed wants the beings of the planet to live in peace. Spirit has been here since the beginning of time, magnificently creating Universes—as it does best—and is working with all of us in our Universe career. Whatever people do is their own expression: to do what they feel helps them feel better in creation, even if, by default, it doesn't really help them feel better.

Spirit allows life to be. Spirit is life. Without Spirit, we wouldn't be.

To be or not to be is the answer to a lifelong question. What a miracle to even be.

Just feeling the heart is Spiritual, for that is our connecting point, energy current, capacity capsule, conduit box.

Whatever is experienced through the heart is Spiritual.

In life, spear it how you want.

Live how you want to live, but remember:

Spirit is and wants all our highest, deepest, and greatest best, and provides all life with endless possibilities.

God's Love Is Beautiful

The world's fate rests upon beauty.
The Spirit of love, truth, and beauty will always admire our Earth.

Children of Light and Love

We are the children of the planet and the souls made by an infinitely Divine Creator, powerful in all ways. We, the souls of this Universe, know that all our challenges can strengthen our abilities for even more compassion, empathy, and devotion to love for the good of all.

We give our hearts and honor life in a sacred way. We gather together in life, learning to love and protecting each other's hearts as best as we can. We acknowledge the courage it took to say yes to a contract of being on Earth, to fly through space, and to step foot out of a womb and onto this planet to experience living as a Spiritual being on a young, evolving planet.

We see the love that guides our way to our destinies. We bow to love and the Angelic orders and the Angelic presences not visible to the eyes but very visible through the transparency of the Divine Spirit within our hearts. We grow for all beings. We live humbly and are grateful for our lives. We learn true fulfillment and peace. We are on this planet with the purest interest and deepest and highest Divine blessing with our optimal, optimized optimism, wishing peace for the hearts of all the people of the planet.

We wish that good, healthy food and good cleansing brings good health to all. We wish for natural, renewable, clean ways for people to live their lives, for the cleansing of the planet, and we hope for all souls the most important love in whatever life may bring.

We know a Spiritual age on the planet is coming!

It is near.

Love is the Doorway

Life is all about receiving information,
and it is all for the purpose of love.

We are all gathering and receiving lots of
information for a special purpose.

It is simple.

Love is the doorway and the key.

Your Master Awaits You

Once you realize you are created by God, the Master of the Divine Universe in the university of Angels, and that you are a being who is realizing the world is surrounded in light, and you are here as a messenger of an understanding of peace in a village of your brothers and sisters, giving all you can to be more and more nurturing and in touch with your higher self to manifest the most important and special purpose of your life for yourself and others, then you see God's beauty in all the struggles of the gravitational experience, and see and feel the magnetic pull toward paradise and the paradise within you, and you emerge from the confusions of the mind and blossom abundantly clear within your heart, the heart of hearts, the gold of the Universe's infinite love, and you know your company is here with the Angels. Then you are the master of your heart and the creator of your life and the observer of God's mysterious, magical, enriching, masterful creation, and you bow your heart in humbled service to the Master of the Universe.

This is very simple for you, and you are now realizing this is your destiny.

For Love I Write

I write for the upliftment of the world.
Why else?

Presence of Peace

If people really knew God's presence in the world, they would live in a way of knowing they were surrounded by an angelically unconditional, Divine Love. Realizing this also brings them the awareness that they can emanate it within themselves, co-creating a world of peace.

Peace falls from the ashes of our love. Love falls from the clouds of our hearts.

Let us drink; let us toast to eternal love.

Gratitude

Fall in love with a thousand things in a day, or even just one. It is a powerful way to live and feel. What a beautiful experience to love so much. The heart holds so much love. All the love within the Universe is wanting, and patiently waiting within you, to be discovered.

I Fell in Love

I fell so deep in love. So deep. So completely, spontaneously, interdimensionally, magically, and mystically deep. Some day you will meet this amazing force, or maybe you already have. She is so amazing—what a God-dess creator to be at the temple of her love. The whole of the Universe is the playground of her love. Unconditionally she prevails beyond time and space. My love will always be with this amazing soul of all souls. The bringer of good is at the table of her love. The taste of her nectar is eternally sweet, infinitely warm, empathetically beautiful, and is the vastness of love and consciousness.

God is male, female, Angelic—call it what you will. It is every molecule in the Universe seen by the eye and is completely and incomprehensibly loving.

The Key to Enlightenment

Enlightenment is the realization that we need to keep our hearts open and keep meditating throughout the rest of our lives.

Life doesn't really end. Life goes on beyond death of the body. So we must embrace the innermost workings of the heart and the Universe as much as we can.

Enlighten the Spirit within Your Being

Life is the mystical, magical synchronizations of love and the mystery spark that is ever-increasing, the Spirit spark that plugs us into its universal, galactivated core show of Divine awakenings of life's experiences!

Every day is a day to awaken within your own enlightenment and become more compassionate, clear, refreshed, nourished, loved, adored, honored, respected, elevated, spiritualized, galactivated, magnetizing yourself toward the way you want to feel and be in the world.

Ultimate enlightenment. I have said to others I don't really use that word too much, because daily living has variable circumstances that are present in the flow of life's fluctuations. The word enlightenment is a very interesting word for me and others. I think some people may feel overwhelmed or not good enough, or so far from it when they hear the word sometimes, because it may seem unattainable, and we might not ever know, in our lifetime on Earth, truly what it is fully until it is felt, experienced, and received into the energy temple of our bodies, minds, and souls.

I feel enlightenment is a daily experience to attain, really, moment by moment; we choose what to do in every circumstance that comes to us.

We choose to enlighten ourselves to do the best that we can do in our day-to-day lives.

So reach for your own ultimate enlightenment in your day-to-day life, and let that be your guide.

Give thanks for the day! You are alive!

Divine Love

Divine Love will always keep shattering your heart open

over and over again until the shining galactic pieces of your heart become diamonds, falling gently into your hands to freely give away.

Opening through the Shattering Heart

The heart will shatter to remain opened. The grinding and crushing days going by will eventually soothe you and will turn into your own soil, which will be refreshed. They will grow the abundant gardens of new mornings of beauty for the workshop of your Divine heart.

You will realize you are in God's sun, sitting in the forests of the Divine Universe. You will feel so calm and at peace, as though experiencing a calm death or rebirth, enough to drift off into that enlightenment. And when you wake up from that meditative dream, you awaken holding your own heart. Here you realize that the Universe is within your very own heart and rests gently within you. It's within you always, like the calm wind of God's own breath before your very own eyes. Your once-shattered heart eventually heals and turns into a bright, shining, golden light— your own best friend—to feel and to look at after all the days of seeking and wondering that you have done in your life, looking all around the world to see if God and his/her treasures truly exist.

The Universe will reach for you; it created you, and you must reach too! See the beauty in all you've been through.

Look deeply within in silent meditation, and remember to look deeply within the specks and shimmers of light within your own fellow beings' eyes. Reflect the great showers of Divine Love and light from the flickering stars of the mystical and magical Universe.

So remember, if your heart breaks, it's just opening up like the lotus, starting you on your new yogi or yogini training journey, closer to your internal home. It is reminding you to fill your heart with that bliss of meditation, and through that practice, naturally you will find God and have great strength and an ever-new joy and understanding in the new quest in your life.

Wellness in mind, body, and soul.

When you break, shatter, cry, be ready for your ever-new joy. The Angels are with you.

Ever-new joy.

You may not always be in a seemingly happy-feeling circumstance, but being content in your heart of hearts, with a trust within the Universe and with an expanding, grateful heart in this gravitational experience, is worth a thousand lifetimes.

Pure Intention

We awaken a little more every day.

Every day we can be reborn in our intention
of the good, the light and the love.

 *Healing*

So much healing in the world is happening right now.

Can you feel it? Can you feel it? Can you feel it?
Can you feel it? Can you feel it?

The ocean of feelings, the waves of our love.

Can you feel it? Can you feel it? Can you feel it?
Can you feel it?

The love for God will sustain you;
nothing else will.

Within My Own Heart is Paradise

I have a sweat lodge, a sacred ceremony, a festival full of yogis and yoginis, a family gathering, a prayer circle, a kumbh-mela*, a tea time with God, a galactivated space launch of my soul, within my own heart everyday.

I wake up and drink tea with God everyday in silent sitting Meditation.

By the time I leave the house, I have already had a party full of light and love.

Sipping the true nectar of Spirit within. A taste of Divine golden honeysuckle molecules of blossoming lotus petals sprinkled with the Universe's essence auric-ly stimulating my every cell throughout my whole body and beyond.

It's within this love that is the doorway and the key.

*Kumbh-mela is a Hindu pilgrimage in which hundreds of millions gather to bathe in the Ganges and Yamuna rivers of India.

Sending Love

Send in your meditations love and light to all going
through hard times. Imagine your people and
the people of the world full of joy.

Instead of being deep in sorrow over the woes of the
world, let us bring ourselves up to see the good
things we are creating in our lives.

Light Will Always Win

Light will always win. Dark is only created as a test by God to see how much we will keep the flame lit within us for good, peace, compassion, and empathy. The light of God is for all who will love the universal Spirit of Love that created all things with love. The Maker of it all just loves whatever is; whatever is not of love falls to the wayside. In the end, love is all that exists. What exists does so because of God and because of unconditional love and goodness. Spirit flows throughout the whole Universe of Universes. Dark is in the world but only because God allows it. Our intentions, optimistic perceptions, and the existence of light can help us transform all things within us, and also see all the good out of any darkness. God can and does transform all things into good a thousandfold. Other worlds may not go through such challenges as we do here on Earth, but perceptions of love with an open heart, and a true knowing of God's love can restore the world back to peace. There is Divine Love always.

I believe this and many people also know this truth. All the great masters, Angels, and helpers of the pure light of God know this.

A Spiritual age is near and yet is here now.

Accomplishments will bring confidence.

Humility will bring success.

 *All One*

We are all children playing on the intergalactic rhythms of life.

All brothers and sisters, different shapes, sizes, and colors.

Going through the same struggles of life and death, the same hopes and dreams, in a desire for deep fulfillment—all the while we watch a few in power run amuck and confuse or brainwash many others.

But we know that we are all family, and we will remain wanting peace for all beings.

Automatically with Spirit

I write for my fun and my own devotion to God, and so that others who read what I write will also be uplifted. Those who are not sure if they know, hear, see, and experience God will at least be uplifted in positive thoughts, feeling more fuller in their hearts and minds, which is the workings of God. So automatically more love and Spirit have been achieved in this full circle to assist others to experience a positive vibration. For those who are reading positive writings with an open heart and mind to experience good vibrations, they will indeed be uplifted, and ultimately will experience God.

 *True Romance*

Only those with a true romance degree in love
feel the supreme beloved.

Ones who have devoted themselves to doing good, with Spiritual
thinking and meditation.

So many flounder at a true Divine romance if distance is
involved. But does God feel distant? Do the Angels feel distant?
Does life feel distant?

Apart of knowing God is in the seeking God. In that seeking we
find a knowing that God's love is everywhere, in all the positive
energies in life.

With deep meditation we relax, breathe and bathe in God's light
and love, knowing the Angels and masters are here with us. The
practice in remembering this love is a tool for the deep knowing
that God's love is always with us.

I sleep with God everynight.

I feel the Angels everyday.

Their hearts are always next to mine. They hear all our desires
and sorrows.

They know our strengths and weaknesses.

We must never doubt the Creator of the Universe.

Whatever troubles are going on,

The Creator has a purpose for all things.

Always try to do good and be good and think of God.

Say to the Creator, "I want to feel your presence. I want to feel all
your love and golden Divine light."

What I know is love will last forever.

A Degree in Love

Until you really know, you'll always wonder. Until you really know if God exists, you will always wonder. The heart-wrenching desire and thirst will bring you your answers, like having all the keys to heaven. What love is here at this gateway, rainbow, opening. Magnify that by 1,000,000,000, and that is God's love for you.

Incomprehensible is this vast ecstasy of God's existence. Wisdom floats on the molecules of love, streams of gratitude, tears, and compassion rain on the high of the heart and soul destined for Spiritual uplifting and real freedom. Awakening masters is the Universe's specialty. Meditation is the fast track for this degree in love.

Ultimate Love

Every day my heart breaks and is filled full with the ultimate and
most satisfyingly unconditional love of the Universe. It is within the
shattering and expansion of my heart that pumps and beats, and within
my lungs that breathe. Spirit never leaves. Beyond the body we receive
deep wisdom, beyond the body we will eventually go.

Universal Love

I love you. You inspire me. The Universe loves you so much.

You're such an amazing being. I believe in you.

Everything is working out for your best and highest good.

You are blessed. Your heart is so pure and full of love.

We all love you so much.

Stay strong in your love for life. You're a child of God.

God is who created the whole Universe, every seed, plant, animal, and human.

God created every butterfly, elephant, and dolphin, and created every Angel and light being.

You are a part of the Angels.

You are a part of God's plan.

You are a miracle being that is made from love.

The most profound essence of love created you.

We are all connected. We are all family. We are all one

Here on this journey together, Brothers and sisters in cosmos of space.

We all are awakening more and more, opening up to hear God speaking within us, gifting us with even deeper feelings of love.

Love is all that is and is all that is of value.

Love is all that truly exists.

You are so loved.

Your birth was so precious.

The Angels watched you being born.

The Creator's love is infinite for you and is always with you, and is for your greatest good.

Remember this now and keep remembering:

You are so loved.

The Earth's Pages of Time

The books and pages in the essence of time are simply the trees and
the planets whispering drops of consciousness molecules, the atoms
and lifetrons, expressing God and all the universal creation, in
all of its magical wonders, Divine Angelic supreme
perfection, diverse beauty and love.

The Still Moments of Time

Everything is a part of God's Creation. In the Matrix, in the slow fragmented moments, it is set up in the stillness for your eyes to observe and see. It is the picture of a picture, to remind you that this is a dream within the dream of reality. This is God's dream, God's movie, God's Creation. It is set up to humble you and to bring you closer to love.

The fractals, particles, molecules, and lifetrons, are the beams of light reminding you of your true home with God. In service to humanity, we work for the good of all; we work for the good of God.

We all play our part, and the role will roll on and keep going. The roles of this play of destiny will play out. The play of this destiny show will go on. The show of God's love will always light the stage and will always be the beautiful end with a new beginning to a new chance to be reborn within eternity.

The Angels and God and the unlimited amounts of God's love are with you.

You are blessed and blessed ever so much greater in your deep openness and awareness of this truth. The truth is that God's love does exist and is the ultimate state of peace to experience.

Universal Play

Whatever we do in life, we know family and the heart are the
T in the Tree of Life. From there we go back to there, now
and then again. Stretching open, expanding the heart. It's our
beginning, our start, our sacred art. The bigger picture of all
that is. The love that binds, bonds and always gives.

The Universe's playground.

You Are Never Alone

You are never really alone because your Angels and guides are always near you, no matter how much you believe or wonder if they are or not. Just how I have been reminded to remember that "everything is energy" by my teachers or my own higher self, I am here sharing this with you now.

I am not your guide but just a friend helping you to remember who you are. I greatly hope to share some inspiration with you and remind you of the miracle that you are in the fabric of the Universe, in the creation made up by molecules created by the Divine unconditionally loving Creator that has many associates to help share the essence of love and Divine Love always. You are truly so loved in this dream of reality beyond your perceptions and comprehensive ability.

What joy it is to have a good time enjoying our own heartbeats and our own souls in the soul of creation that is powerfully guiding our own selves toward the deep healing and gratitude within self-realization and God realization.

Feel the Miracle

The miracle of life is already settled in every cell of your being; it's in your bones.

You are the miracle. It's up to you to feel it.

All life and creation in all the Universe is related to you.

You are a family member to all the stars in the cosmos.

You are related to everything. Love is infinite. Beyond what you believe, the Angels, the Universe, God, are all holding you as a child of creation.

You are loved dearly.

Always Time for Great Remembrance

You want what is glamorous, but what is more glamorous than knowing God?

Look at the sparkles of eternity in the stars in the sky and the endless answers granting wishes to all the galaxies of galaxies.

You want attention, but who else can give you more attention than you?

You are the one who is capable of loving yourself more than anyone.

You want to heal, but do you give yourself time to rest?

You have the power to be humble and ask God to help you in your situation.

You seek freedom, so why do you stay caged in all your pain, deep worries of the future, and self-doubt?

You give so much time for everything else, but do you ever just sit in deep meditation with yourself and God?

You may wonder, "What can sitting in silence do for me? I am overweight and need exercise, or I am worried about how to make money because I have none and need to find work, or I have money but still I am not happy in my life. I am still not sure what my purpose is." So, I say to you now from the Angelic broadcasting station: That is the best time to meditate and talk to God in silence.

Give your heart to the Creator, and send your love to the Angels and feel their love all around you. It is the perfect time to put your hand on your heart and feel all the love you have inside yourself and connect with your own vessel/space-traveling device. Imagine the Angels around you. It is the greatest time to ask the Angels to be around you and walk with you wherever you go, and to give you the strength to manifest all your dreams to come true or whatever is for the best and highest good.

Imagine a blanket of light all around you. Feel a big force of love all around you. Know that the trees, the sun, moon, and stars are always with you. Remember that you are always loved unconditionally by the Universe. Remember that your pain and tears will wash away and bring you more empathy for others and great wisdom for the children to come. Remember the joy that is building and budding so full within you like the most amazing lotus flower, because you are getting closer and closer to your higher self and God, in this moment and for all moments to come.

You are beginning to remember that it is here, in this deep silent sitting meditation, that you are drinking tea with God, bringing even more life force energy to your brain and whole being, bringing yourself more light and positivity, charging yourself up, full with love, more and more, in this deep self-love with God. Realize this is your home, also, in this space, and no matter what the troubles of the world, you can come here any time and send love to all beings, feeling calm, relaxed, and so full of love. From this point on, we create our dreams. From this practice, our purpose comes from here, from this deep love in the gratitude of life and love, for all that is good, and all we *are* that is good and all we can *do* that is good.

We are grateful; we are loved; we are blessed; we are nourished, nurtured, honored, received, and so humbled by Love.

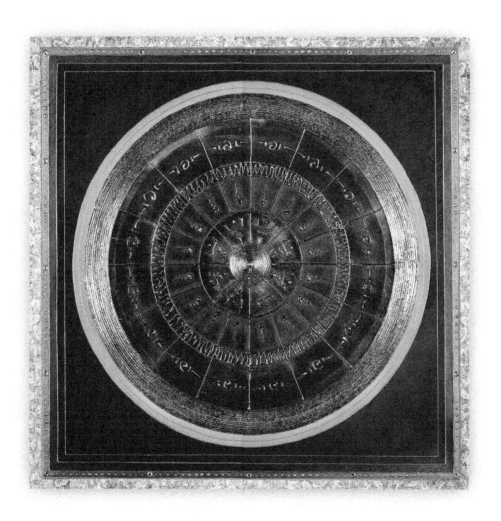

Just Sit

The way to meditate for more silent sitting hours is to meditate more silent sitting hours. It is not a question of how much you stretch or how flexible you are to sit longer. Just sit. Sit comfortably, and do it daily.

Love is the Doorway and the Key

I am a light being, always moving, always seeing, always changing, always singing, always giving and receiving.

Giving light, letting go, experiencing the heart, mind, body, and soul.

Teaching others, living grace, floating merkaba right in space.

Intuition, looking in, bliss, joy, from within.

Meditation, steady pace, Divine courage, giving space.

Divine Love, blessings always, the Universe always holds me.

Seeking heaven from within, Divine Love, let it spin.

Jamaica, Greece, Brazil, Australia, to the Middle East, ending hunger, creating peace.

Healing Earth, giving birth, clean soil, good seeds, lots of water, basic needs, Angelic light we are taken, holy presence, the Master's making.

A Spiritual age is coming soon, feeling magic, Earth, moon, feeding the hungry with a spoon.

We are spreading love to demonstrate, making leaders, dissolving hate, hearts pounding, core grounding, music playing. I'm just saying.

Galactivation for the nation, universal love integration, blowing it up on your YouTube station, the holy voice of creation.

One love is this new sensation. So if you are in meditation, now you are having God-realization.

Contemplate, meditate, spreading light, dissolving hate, feeling love, never without, that's what yoga's all about.

Spine straight, energy flowing, visions created, Spirits knowing, compassionate self, hearts glowing. This love never ends. It's my heart, galactic heart, that mends, opening chakras when the body bends. Angelic light-beings are my holy friends, universal love my heart extends, when I'm turning on my Divine, Angelic, 3-D vision Spirit lens, knowing that mystically, magically,

Love is the doorway and the key.

For Love I Write

Silent meditation and writing
eventually go hand in hand.
Or should I say hand and heart.

Realization into a Deep Love

Imagine if everyone you ever met or knew is an incarnation of you! That our hearts are vibrating together and that in the fabric of the Universe in time and space and in a dimension of all that is possible, all whom you meet are you, just in a different body in time. Ah, what compassion comes out of this realization, and what joy comes into being for the deep love for all beings!

When realizing Spirit is in all, it seems the word Spiritual can be misunderstood by the ego of self within the floating Universe. We may say "I am Spiritual. I am a good person. I do my inner work. I live in a Spiritual way." The bigger picture is that Spirit dwells deep within all. Spirit u all.

Not everyone chooses to be good or nice in the world. Discernment of who we choose to be around is always a good thing.

Gentle Strength

Strengthen the love you have in your own heart
for the Creator, the Angels, your guides, your inspirations,
and the rest will follow.

Green Essence

Universe, I love your natural parts. Your lips of nature-green, gum-drop, gob-stopper colors of healing green leaves, your hips of deep natural beauty that is wholly you, in my eyes. Your tips and grey roads and streets only paint a shade of your aura on the shade cloth of your essence, your vegan outfits, your fire, meditation, and yoga studios.

O, may you be redeemed in my perception and uplifted in my meditations, remembering always that my deep nature meditations always give me strength, bringing in that great light of compassion and deeper wisdom when I relight the torch of my soul. Knowing God's existence, the Angels and the light beings are always with and within me, in the forefront of my soul, and offering that knowing up to all the cities.

I love the quiet calm nature of this Earth.

Always new roads traveled.

The Power of Love

Strengthen your ability to bring power and attention to your heart
through your breath and relaxation in meditation,
and your mind will follow in devoted service to the Spirit, your heart,
and the unconditional Divine Love within the Universe.

Happy ThanksLiving Day

I am grateful and thankful for living on this ThanksLiving Day.

I am thankful for this life, this breath, in the depth of my soul. I am thankful that Spirit can break all barriers of mind and calmly reside in the luscious paradise of the body temple. I am thankful and grateful that within each person there is something special, something uniquely created by the Divine Mother and Father of all. I am thankful that in this world, in the dream of reality, there is room for great highs in the supreme Divine Love within the heart, that the Earth is a place where much is possible, that the Creator has created us and sent the Angels to be within us and all around us. I am thankful for the shadow of negativity, for it has shown the great and bright light of positivity into my view. This light of God and the Universe glows so gently, spiraling each soul in unconditional love. I hold this in my heart every day, from this now to all the nows to come.

I am in supreme gratitude for all experiences that are felt, good or bad. Breaking into the deep love of the Universe, feeling held, nurtured, blessed, and received, with all my needs met. All the miracles are right here in my life, in my body and inside my being. All love is within my heart and is flowing from the same current, the same waves of God's ocean of joy from the Angelic realms of paradise. So humbly and deeply blessed we all are. Eating or not eating, sleeping or not sleeping, just simply being and even able to breathe at all.

I attest that every day I wish all the love in the Universe to flow right into your heart, up through your spine, into your brain, and back out up through the Universe, leaving you with the full knowing in your life experience about the very real energy currents of God's great light that are always within your being.

Lift Yourself & Fly

Learn to lift yourself up in a good way,
a loving, caring, open way.
Open yourself up to having love for all beings in the Universe,
and the Angels will gift you with your own wings.

Inner Peace and Love

Your inner peace will reach for you. You must also reach for it.

Daily meditation will bring you the inner peace and happy heart that you seek. This inner peace is fully available for those who choose to experience it.

The unassuming mind rests, calm and tranquil, in love and light, while gathering bits of wisdom in the warmth of self-love, in the Divine university of Angels, and in the unconditionally loving Universe.

All wings on deck while you perform for God, dropping deep into your heart, clearing your pains and sufferings, showing your love, calling in your guides, blasting your self with the golden light of the Universe in a blanket of hopes, riding the waves on your magical carpet in Divine ecstasy, loved, adored, nourished, nurtured, blessed, honored, received, and humbled by love.

Daily meditation, there is nothing like it. It is its own thing and has its own benefits beyond comprehension.

When you are ready, your higher self will be waiting.

A Love So Deep

One whose love runs so deep in honor, loyalty, and devotion
to the divinity of Angelic perception
will provide an unbreakable rhythm to the chorus of love.

Awakening masters of love is the Universe's specialty.

The word love is uncovering the mysteries of time.

Love and God are the same,

learning love is our daily practice.

Resting into Our Love

Opening up to the presence of the moment and the presents of our hearts when sitting or standing in nature, we may take deep interest, from the belly of our breath, into the life and the life plasma of the tree. We can observe the swaying body of the tree in the wind. We can see the shape and curves of its presence, so gentle, in all of its strength. Learning all about its rhythms, its needs, its voice, its message, its life cycle, in the calm, soft, and short timeless moments, in the whisperings of its leaves.

Taking notice into our hearts and into the candy-blue sky, the voice within gives us the chance of lifetimes to remember, once more, the Spirit and the golden, Divine openings of the heart. In one moment we observe the wisdom of eternity in the ethers of time. In one moment we experience the clear knowing that, throughout all the openings of the heart, throughout all our life cycles, there is always more and more room for more and more compassion and love. The heart sometimes feels as if it is open all the way! to the very limit! bursting open into the Divine ecstasy! Other times, it feels hollow, like a tin can, hard, numb, and all used up.

Even in these moments we can choose to see the true value in life, seeing the best viewpoint we have ever chosen to see yet! We can choose even in this now! We can receive the innermost special blossomings of the heart, with this message even being in our deepest gratitude for our tour through space, for our very own Earth body, space body, our very own Earth home, in this spacetime. Full of resources in the now of forever-expanding love and all the abundance that comes within that miracle! Being in gratitude for all of our lives, our breath, our bodies, and our

Spirit, and again to our very own openings in the surrendering to Spirit! Knowing that there is always the true home within the heart of hearts, the knowing that we will never be without the great Spirit.

We devote this moment, this breath, this time in our lives as the true warriors of light to move forward, allowing our hearts to burst open regularly in the fabric of the Universe. So acceptable, vulnerable, and sustainable, we open up, calm, nourished, loved, grateful, and blessed. Knowing that we are being guided, only and absolutely by love! The higher self, the Spirit, the Earth, the Angels, the Universe, God.

To all my relations, to all people, to all tribes.

Aho!

Growing in Fulfillment

May all things grow in a good way as they do, completely
enhancing your heart-awareness of where the Spirit gem
sits, growing and becoming closer to your higher self,
seeing a life of Divine Love within your heart, the quest
and the entrance to your very own paradise within.

Paradise is also within You

I am sorry to tell you this, but it is inevitable that the Mother Earth will lay you back down again, straight to the ground and to her feet.

The worldly confusions may sway you and leave you with a heavy heart and a used-up body, indeed. Your heart may remember too much pain, yet still not enough to take you to your knees to pray and meditate daily.

But you must relax and know your heart is safe; no one can take it but Spirit, and Spirit is what gives you all your strengths, sufferings, and experiences.

So just imagine the possibilities of what is to come.

An unimaginable and ultimately unconditional, intriguingly mystical, potently magically Spiritual, not-yet-experienced, sublimely subliminal, exceedingly and over-surpassingly, astoundingly astonishing, unannounced encounter with your blissfully, masterfully, all-embracing God that is inside you, that is always in the now, always and forever, Divinely available in you, with a surprise that you may not even know that you crave, giving you exactly what you need at every moment, whispering in your ears to tell you to listen up and start meditating, and the life-spark energy and the magnificent joy and content in your heart from it will sustain your every cell until the day you fly with your Angel friends to the next journey toward more unfathomable beauty and love, surrounding all the beings there that are infinitely connected and created like you, that have also come to and experienced the Universe and world like you have.

Sooooo blessed, right?

Look deep within you for your highest love and light.

Ask the Angels to be with you; they will guide.

Universal Blessings

Our gifts and talents are blessings from the Creator!

Never shun these gifts.

Love all the good you do!

Love all your gifts!

Being able to feel gratitude for what we have

and love for what we do in the world

puts more love into the air!

The Seeking Little Throbbing Heart

What is it that you want, that you think God can't give you?

What is the true key to your heart? The key to heaven?

What is it that the Divine has not shown you yet? Tell me?

Because once you have found what your heart has always been seeking, then that is when you find what you are looking for.

So you see?

God has created you!

You are the only one like you!

You are a miracle made by the infinite, and you have infinite potential.

The ecstasy from lots of meditation is like no other. I tell you this:

More ecstasy than the greatest desire — one hundred million times that.

Through meditation is a true ecstasy, and God will find you, but you must seek Him/Her/the Creator Master, that is also within you.

So you must meditate. Meditate. Meditation is very powerful.

Just little prayers won't do. Sincere prayer is always good. So go deep into it. Go deep into meditation.

Once a month, once a week, pull yourself away from the world and meditate many hours, or just a half hour or an hour a day at first.

God will fulfill you. I promise you that.

You must know that God will fulfill you. Remember this.

This is God's show.

So watch the miracles unfold, and don't be so caught up in the movie.

For it's not about the movie.

The world right now may seem sad with wars and troubles, ignorance and despair.

But God doesn't want that for you.

You are in the world and not of it, and if you seek the Divine, then the Universe, the Great Spirit, will show you the ocean of love.

You will see everything differently — so beautifully — and you will see and feel the whole of all creation. You will see only the magnificence, and your new job will be to try to embrace all the greatness that was created for you.

You will see the Great Light,

and you will realize that you can perform in life with all the great love of the cosmic ocean and create the destiny you want,

and, at the same time, still not be of the world.

This is the true bliss. You will feel great joy and be full of Divine Love.

So abundant you will feel. God is with you and God loves you.

Remember this now. Thank you. Feel the light of the Angels. They are with you. All the great Masters are with you. Become a Spiritual alcoholic. Meditate.

OOOOMMMM

The Strongest and Fittest

Being healthy is always a good thing.

To me, life isn't about who is the strongest and fittest.

To me, it's about who has the openness to cultivate a gentle, Divine understanding of love

and compassion for all beings!

Returning to the One Source

Everyone is now becoming, or will eventually become, a yogi or yogini. It is only a matter of time.

The light of the stars are all connected.

At some point in this life or the next, you will go deep within in silent sitting meditation and ride the calm waves of Divine Love in the temple of your own heart and at the feet of God—Love. Even now, as you peacefully sleep at night, you are connected to the omnipresent of all that is, resting in that bliss. You are never far away from God. You are always in God's presence and always so very close to the practice, to practicing the presence of God.

There are tools to feel better in this life, settling deeper into the paradise of Divine Love. This life energy that runs through your spine, your body, your brain, is the light energy of Love—God. Your existence itself is beaming out and emanating the light of the Universe particles and the breath of life in creation. You are all the children of creation, a part of all the billions of galaxies within the Universe. The Angels are working with all to lift us up, to walk softly and compassionately on this Earth. We are all made from star dust. How blessed we all are to live in the miracle of life.

Your Own Heart

Your heart is your greatest gift.

More and more, your heart expands throughout your entire life, revealing the wonders of love and all the great mysteries.

By keeping our hearts open.

True Brilliance

We are all brilliant in our own ways. Just look around you; God is expressing the magnitude of the brilliance of life every day in everything and in every cell of your being.

You exist — that in itself is brilliant and magical. What a gift this life is. Day in and day out, above and below, we watch eternity in every moment while the Earth spins in harmony with space. I feel my own brilliance lies in calming the brain to drop deeper into the heart of hearts.

Inner peace.

That, to me, is true success.

A Unique & Inimitable Faith

Lift your Spirits. Life is about showing the Creator that
you will pick yourself back up through all your challenges
and look up to the heavens and still say thank you.

It is about showing the inimitable faith through your
human experience, that you believe the Divine will
always bless you, even if you sometimes doubt the
Divine Mother and Divine Father.

Surrender to the Path of Meditation

Keep reading, thinking, and studying your own mind, your own heart, life, and the Universe, and when you realize that you cannot comprehend all of the magical, mystical miracles of the Divine Universe, then you will realize that you are ready to meditate and go deep into a different bliss—a bliss of clarity, which includes expansiveness; healing, energizing, revitalizing showers of love. Then you will blanket yourself more and more with that frequency of love, the flowing lotus blossom of your heart and mind. The greatest gift. The transmutation closer to your heart of hearts. The uncovering of all the great wisdom within you, with all the great Masters working with you.

You will see. When you are ready. The Universe is patient; your higher wisdom is patient; we are patient. But know it is always your time to choose and remember who you are, and that you are loved very much by many in the Universe.

In time, the clouds of the mind will be wiped away
with the practice of silent meditation,
and the sun will shine down on you
like a peace from heaven.

The Angels are with you!

The Time is Now

What is a thousand years?
If it is all a part of the time that is right now.

Now, now, now, now . . .

Good Visions

I think and know and feel, intuitively and logically, that the world will be okay. In the end there will be a beginning. All will see everything with a new insight. An internal love and knowing of Divine Love of the Creator and the Angels will be stronger than ever before. This time will bring all souls together in Divine unity, the Angelic vision that the Angels have had since the beginning of life on the planet Earth.

All will be well. All is perfectly imperfect. All will be well in time. Time heals all. We are on a young, evolving planet with evolving souls. We are brave. Being on Earth, we are learning courage and strengthening our souls in a new way.

All will be revealed in time. Time heals all. There is a master plan, truly. Wake up to see the bigger picture. That's all we can do, really. Be of kind nature. Help each other as best we can. We are all related. Gratitude for the air we breathe, the water and food we eat, and the Spirit of love we experience within our hearts. Many are going through many challenges: emotional, physical, and financial.

Empathy, empathy, empathy.

Infinitely Clear

Infinitely clear, like a clear glass of water. Depending on the angle
of the observer, the water may not be visible to the eye. This is
how God, the Spirit, the Angels, would seem to the unobserver.

What angle are you looking from?
Look all around and in your own heart.
Meditation may help you see more clearly.

Be easy on yourself, but do try and start your silent
meditation practice for your own heart.

A Cup of Upliftment

Ask yourself when you start your silent meditation: What is in the flow between me and God?

May we let the calm soothing awareness of relaxation in silent meditation drift within every cell of our own being to give us all the answers. It may sound like this.

Just breathe. Just love. Just be.

The brain may want to try to go into the battlefield of thoughts and concerns, but dim it away from there! Let God do all the fixing of the world in the Angelic realms! May we also take the time to relax and enjoy ourselves in the temple of our own self-love and the love of God's presence. Spend time, an hour or more a day, sipping tea with God in silent meditation.

No need to work our brains and our bodies to death; your body and mind on Earth are temporary as it is, so that is inevitable.

You may ask, Well, what is meditation? What is it for?

Meditation is one of the keys in life. It is not like gambling with yourself, it is always beneficial. You could say it is like a game and that if you play with it, you will always win the greatest rewards!

Your heart will tune in and realize that if you treat yourself and the people in your life with loving care and upliftment as you would a young child, there will always be a better outcome.

We should always try to remember to not let the stresses of the day take away from our ability to be in a calm and caring place. We do have a choice.

Divine Love Always

Beyond the worries of your mind, your higher wisdom, your guardian Spirit of your heart and soul, brings to you the soothing presence of all the love and wisdom of the Universe. It sits at your feet, waiting for you in a calm, warm, luscious paradise, and is omnipresent within you, deep in a Divine whispering silence, all around you and in everything, waiting for you to join in on the party with your silent meditation practice.

Are you coming?

On the Days of New

In deep meditation, three suns had fallen. I suddenly fell so deep in the Divine that my soul wanted nothing else than the quiet solitude of my own heart, the peace and self-love and tranquility from the electrifying realizations and feelings of God's presence, the temple of pyramids and the Divine golden light, the shedding of tears and the supreme knowing and ecstatic bliss of such an occasion with the omnipresent, all-pervading light and love.

Nothing could hold me back from this encounter, for I had endured too much pain from the dream nightmare of the world. All of my being is ready and in gratitude, meeting the cellular waves of my passing and eternal life. The final spiral up; my body weightless to all before me and all to come.

The heart carries the spheres of space, the Universe in time, the God in every moment, the lifetimes of new unfolding, the Angelic pathways, the key to the door of miracles, the full surrender and increasingly dense desire for the Divine.

When it feels that Spirit is using your fingers to produce a masterpiece, that is a good feeling.

Even Yogis Embrace Great Change

Even yogis get overwhelmed sometimes, and even super yogis do too. Gushing the heart deep in solitude within the calm relaxations and bliss waves of omnipotent spiraled sparks of love, there can still be big concern for the world and seeing the real suffering of the people. Sad things happen in the world all the time, causing the Heart to be drenched at the feet of tears and emotion. Love wings are lit with the torch of God's light and love.

Remembrance that this life is always God's house no matter what it seems. This includes the Universe's love trails, and the pathways of every valley. It even includes every curve of our body and brain, and even up our spine and back out to everything that exists. Even the super yogi has the want to want nothing but knows that the desire is to want and wish for world peace and the inner happiness for all the world's peoples and all beings that have ever been and all those yet to come. Even the yogi cries tears. Even the yogi feels pain. Even the one who seems closest to God has trials and tribulations and great learning and deep thoughts of the beauty of the afterlife. The yogi loves. The yogi breaks and bends. The yogi knows what you're going through and is here for the rising of the frequencies of all mortals and the healing of the planet. Claim your love and stand strong with it.

Clearing the Mind

You brush your teeth because you want to keep your teeth
clean, beautiful, and healthy, right?

You clean your body, you clean your car, you clean
your dog, and you clean your toilet even, so why don't
you meditate? Don't you want your brain to be clean,
beautiful, and healthy, too?

Is it just your teeth, your body, your car, your dog,
and your toilet that you want to be clean?

We also need the cobwebs and dust of the mind
to be cleaned away.

Indeed!

Life Fulfillment

To realize and be fully functioning in the Divine realm and bliss of creation is not just to learn to remember equations or follow a curriculum to exercise the muscle of the brain, but to immerse ourselves in the clear space of meditation, being able to edit and watch our thoughts as they come in and out, and, at the same time, relax in the Divine bliss of the eternal love of our higher selves.

This is where the highest life fulfillment settles in.

Laugh with Love

Laugh in the face of your personal stories.
The real reality is God's existence.

This is not a religious phenomenon.
It just simply is.

Let this be your opening.
Relax and take it in!

Breathe.

Time for Beauty

No matter how things are going in life or how it seems, practice expanding your love more and more with the love that is truly all around you, always when in silent sitting meditation or in your daily waking life.

Hold the vision that you are surrounded in light and love with all your family, dearest friends, guides, and greatest Spiritual teachers, and that they are with you, always.

Live in the presence of your own heart. Let that be your present. Everything in life that seemed impossible to you before becomes possible through silence and the integration of more love in deep, silent sitting meditation.

This is also where you will hear your own heart sing about the open doors of the Universe. Silent meditation is a beautiful practice worth learning.

Focus, concentrate your mind. Practice regularly.

Gift from Your Own Heart

Focus on what you do love, not on what you don't,
and the warmth of Spirit will always fill your body and soul
with the gifts and prayers from your own golden temple that
were polished and held sacred by your own loving heart.

God's Movie

We are all stars in God's movie! Are you a star or an extra?

Are you still a victim of life's circumstances, or are you giving energy to your expansion and healing to your inspirational self, and using that energy to realize the vastness of the Universe's love for you? Are you every day living in gratitude and moving forward as an empathic, caring being who hopes and envisions the planet in love and light and holding a deep compassion for all beings?

Change is Inevitable

Change is what life is, needs, and creates to evolve into the newness of the mystical, magical mystery that always is and will always be present within God's Divine miracles.

Life Is, You Are, God Is, Love Is

Life is not just some fairy tale with beautiful skies and sunsets, waterfalls and valley views. It is also full of dirty socks, cold blankets, broken hearts, and bad news, but that's also the beauty, and it is the Creator of love's design, for whatever reason. There are miracles, Angels, fairies, many light beings beyond the curtain, and that is also very real. Work on your own self, your own self-love, your gratitude, your desire to allow good into your life, your willingness and ability to remain discerningly open with your heart and open to consciousness. Receive the bits and pieces of information of universal love, and see the success in having the access to all the love right in your own heart and at your fingertips. There, in that space, in the simplicity of your very own never-ending bliss supply, overflows your golden nectar of Divine Love.

God is love. Love is God. And it is that light energy that created the Earth, all the galaxies in the Universe, you, and all the beautiful magic you can ever imagine.

So give thanks. Show your respect. Practice being in the presence of God. Meditate a little bit every day, once a week for many hours, or once a month. Show your love and go deeper in your own self-love, whatever that may be for you. Remember to meditate. You are so loved, beyond words, beyond your thoughts or dreams. In the wisdomatic thought-waves of love.

Wisdom beyond thought.

Despair Can Be Like a Slingshot

With our supreme desire and courage,
we can shoot back out to the stars.

The World is Waking Up

May we look up to all the great Masters and people who are peacefully aware and practicing to love more compassionately toward all hearts here on the planet. May all people realize that God is love and love is the true religion. May all people realize that the great masters of compassion in the past taught to love our fellow human beings, and may we aspire to be great, compassionate, and aware ourselves. May the people of the world stop fighting about which name of the master Creator of the Universe is the best name and the true name. God is great no matter what name you give to God or what you believe in to describe Divine Love. The Angels are always with us and want us all to love all beings.

Religions of the world, please teach the people who come to learn from you to be compassionate and loving, and love each other as brothers and sisters.

Respect Love

Respect love, and love will bow with you.

Open up your heart and love becomes your mystical
and magical playground, leading you inevitably
to find all the keys to Heaven's doors.

You Are the Champion of Your Own Life

If your desires have you in a chokehold, remember God is the referee. Listen to the whistle. The blows of the world have their limits. How much are you willing to suffer?

Listen to the inner voice. God will never steer you wrong, but you must know the rules and your limits. Train hard. Find healing with yourself or a light worker. Go deep in meditation, and you will always be the champion of your life. You are the master of your life. Humble yourself deeper in Divine Love and the light of devotion. Do your inner work.

Angels Whisper

Meditation is the downloading of the Divine and the Angels
through the ethers of time. The primitive tribunals of the past
have nothing to do with the Angelic realm. Let things go.
The details of human life, the day in and day out, are just the
short journeys for the soul evolution, gaining more realization
of God's love before the mystical, magical journey ahead!

A surprise beyond wonder or imagination.

World Peace

We are happy when others are happy. When the people we love smile or laugh, we naturally have a feeling of peace. When people have their basic needs met and have food, water, and shelter, we all feel good. We all want that for everyone.

We have the wisdom from the great beings that have come to our Earth for the special purpose of sharing about Spirit, the care we all could have for one another, and the information of where we came from, what we are doing here, and where we are going. That information should be shared to the people of the Earth and in our schools, etc. So finding the keys to life's simple truths is crucial for oneself, the community, and the global community for world peace.

Divine Perception

Are you a part of the corruption in the world?

Or a part of a world of solutions and universal achievements?

Loving Message

Life is about experiencing beauty.

We are all expressing a frequency of love in some way.

Every person is living in a warm body made with molecules designed by the Creator of the Universe, a part of the Universe and a part of you.

God will inevitably express the power and unconditional light through all beings.

Religion is not needed for God's power and love to be so.

No matter what people believe or not, no matter the religion people have,

That is not a concern for the Creator.

There will be a rise in the frequency of the planet no matter what the minority of people may think, or the destruction they may attempt to cause for themselves or others [through their inability to care for the Earth and all beings].

Love is the true religion.

I bring the world a message.

I do this for the Creator of all and all the orders of Angelic beings working together in the Universe.

The love in the Universe is great!

So listen up!

Deeply tune in with your heart, with your silent meditation practice, and if you don't have one yet, then make it a priority to have one.

This will help you to clear and shed your pains, judgments, and confusions about your reality

and come to awaken into the reality of the mystical and magical adventure

with the many, many, meditation-practicing yogis and yoginis in the world.

Eternal Values

May we learn to give what we can and may we learn what
that truly is for ourselves in our daily meditations.

Heart Vision

We are all like heart scientists studying the heart, searching its pathways, finding its treasures, its mysteries and wonders, while being televised to all of the Universe.

The Universe's love is infinite in its magnitude, breathtaking, surpassingly nurturing, and the unconditional love can be seemingly unimaginable to the human mind. Your tears will fall in your humility when you experience it.

Meditation is an effective and powerful way to go deeper into the heart, creating more positive shifts in yourself, and sending out a vibration of love all over the world.

A Clear Awakening

The changing and evolving desire of the will, can also work to be of great benefit and strength for all of us who may eventually come out of a Spiritually-deprived coma.

Choosing to love, we look deeper and tap into the soul, realizing that within us all is a unique universal teacher. Your higher self is as glowing and as bright as the brightest stars in the sky, illuminating with so much love and wisdom, destined specifically and uniquely for you.

God is with you, within you, around you, behind you; seek Him/Her/the All, finding all you need.

There you will find true joy.

Meditation is a super key — use it.

More love will be waiting there.

Life Plasma

Silent meditation, a simple little key to dropping deeper into our hearts.

Each time we do it, we are clearing up any emotional pains, illusions of the mind, and wiping away all our material sorrows,

Slowly developing and remembering our higher wisdom,

Learning to embody who we really are: a pure manifestation of Spirit coming into the physical body.

We are temporarily being stationed on the planet to express a true Angelic being within us.

We are now realizing we are here to emerge and be one with our Angels, to vibrate the frequency of love, in the energy and life plasma of our Earth.

With the Angels

We are here with the Angels. We are a part of them. In the bigger picture God does pulse his light through all beings, big and small. We are the children. We can communicate only because of the Angels' presence. Without God, nothing exists. Our thoughts and desires are possible through the Divine Spirit. Pulling us like the moon pulls the waves of the ocean.

We are in the University of Life
Learning about love for eternity

Expansions & Depth

If we choose to wear a devotional robe, a piece of jewelry, have a necklass, or keep a crystal for more good energy or protection may we always be empowered to remember who we are, where we came from and remain fully open to the love within the Universe that is always showering us with God's pure light. We know that we are not the body, we are not the clothes we wear, we are beings within a shell of muscle, bones and molecules wrapped in God's pure light emanating in the Universe. Always striving to do good in all we do. Letting go of thoughts that dont serve us and replacing them with gratitude to enjoy the miracle of life. Are attitude adjustment is are gratitude adjustment. We strive to expand our consciousness out to the Universe and go beyond ritual thinking, beyond religion, beyond everything material in meditation and lay in the hammock of our Divine hearts with God.

We remember we all came into this world naked and then wore diapers. We know we are always helpless babes growing up in the Universe to be closer to God.

Go deep within your heart every chance you get to be in a silent sitting meditation sipping tea with God.

Deep Listening

People talk a lot, yes? Lol, but who is listening?
So many people are driving, but who is
walking in deep contemplation?
So many people reading, but who is meditating hours a day?

Learn to relax and quiet your mind in meditation.
Feel the love you have in your heart.
So much love is in your heart for so many people!
This love is for you to feel; it is a gift.
All wisdom is in your heart, all the universal love
is within your being.
Perennial peace, a daily practice.

Divine Connection

We are connected to all the beautiful people in our lives.

We are the amazing inspirations in our lives. We are full of unconditional love.

There is no separation between us. We are loving people deep within our hearts. We are the trees, the animals, the Earth, and the Angelic beings. With the great realizations in our deep meditations, this is what is revealed,

Helping us all to shed, more and more, any illusion we have to awaken our Divine souls.

Those who we might think have led us farther from our realizations of Divine Love have only created a little obstacle, easily lifted by our enjoyment of and devotion to our daily meditations.

All will work out in your life in the highest good, and love will undoubtedly magnify with your unturned devotion to being in your heart and knowing you are loved by the Universe. Devote more time every day, if you can, to silent meditation.

Life will always sway and bring us little bumps in the road, and eventually the little bumps become fun things to joyfully jump over.

Some challenges are harder than others, and they always help us to get stronger. Challenge yourself, and always keep your heart open.

Meditate, cleanse your body, and eat healthy, practice yoga, exercise, work, play, dance, love, and give to others.

May your life be eye opening to what and who you are and what you love most.

Your Yoga Is Physical

Even if you practice yoga just for physical health, you can still have communion with God: whether you know God, believe in God, or not. When you're stretching, you are doing a physical thing to help the betterment of your body, calming of your emotions and bringing life energy, circulating energy, to your body, your heart, your brain.

In those moments of peace you may realize deep things for yourself and how to even give yourself even more love or even be a better person in the world. That is good.

The yoga taught to me goes deep into the non-physical. Yoga is about the union with God. I go deep within with the intention to sprout the seeds of God's love and the nectar of that sensational bliss within my heart, calling on the Angels, my teachers and masters, light beings, devas of the Earth to be with me, sit with me, live within my heart. I play with the invisible paralyzed in the deep songs of deep silence, unbreakable focus, unwavering understanding of God's love for man and women-kind. I sit in the solitude space of ego-shattering blankets of hope, honeycombed with torpedo-shaped, amber hue, Angelic, glistening light.

My love for God is not just my physical activity, my pose, or my performance of stretches. Some on the planet can't even move their bodies, does that mean they can't do yoga?

God is in all things even in the thoughts you have that are distant from your true future of infinite love that is depending on your time of your awakening to realize all the love is right here with you always.

The Universe breeds Masters out of humans dormant in egoic formation: statues of bodies not fully aware of the Master of their own making. The university of Angels made a wish with the air before air or even your eye lashes were even created for the new life plasma on this planet.

The soul indeed needs and speeds its way closer to the all-knowingness of where it is going this life or the next. Asleep or awake you will reach your home. Home in your illusions, home in your body, home in your breath, your love, home in your heart. Home at the seat of Angels.

Yoga is a practice of the union with God: deep heart opening valuable sequences of your soul with Spirit. Your physical merging with the non-physical, invisible.

The Eyes of Compassion

In the eyes of compassion and deep awareness, we learn many things. One of the things we learn is discernment in the open heart of our love. We cannot judge others if we are wanting to lift them up. We may choose to not do all the things others do because we may not approve of certain decisions others make. To lift others up with deep compassion, we need to have the energy. To help others masterfully, we need to have a deep, gentle approach to express a great love. We are all learning this one. May we prevail in that pure intention of wanting the highest and best for all beings.

Deep Space 9

Dive deeply into the deep space nine of your inner self/higher self in your meditation, and settle into your heart humbly with your intention. Let the Universe know your here to go deeply within. Focus on your breath, relax and set your timer. Let this be your traveling vortex. Other things may serve you in other ways but when you are finally ready for warp speed ahead, with your turbo boosters, into the Universal self, this is the truth, the light, and the way, to reach your destination. You're home in your very own Paradise within. Love is the doorway and the key.

Learn silent meditation and do it daily :)

All is Well

Be one with the answer, not two with the problem.

All can be resolved and restored. Time heals all.

Great wisdom will linger within your universal body, like a key to your heart and to your soul's destiny. You will find it at the golden throne of your silent meditation practice. Opening like a lotus, your heart lets in all the warmth of the sun. Your thoughts are like the waves of the ocean on a peaceful beach. Angelic rays burst through your heart-fire of passion, guiding your energy swiftly back to the light.

Universal Questions

If you could ask the Universe any question, where do you think is the first place your answer would find you?

All the questions you have about life may come to you through your desire to learn, obviously, and all the answers you never expected you would ever get to experience and discover will come to you through your heart and your meditation practice.

Through your meditation practice, you will naturally experience the real bliss of the warm, embracing, all-loving, all-knowing inner wisdom.

Your own heart will expand full of God's love, the Angels' love, the great masters' love, the Universe's love, the Divine Mother Spirit, Jesus, Melchezadec, Buddha, Krishna, Quan Yin, Mother Mary, Babaji, Lihari Mahasai, Sri Yukteswar, Paramahansa Yogananda, and even the fairies, and all beings of pure light. The list goes on!

The Door to Heaven

I live for my meditation. Connecting with
my heart and Spirit is what sustains me.

I love, breathe, and live off of pure Spiritual energy. I love
and live for Divine awakenings for a living. My purpose is
being the greeter at love's door. When you come and arrive
at the door where I sit, I will give you a warm Angelic
blanket of light and lay down a pillow for you to sit on to
meditate, to feel all the love within your heart, so that when
you enter the kingdom of heaven, your heart is already
familiar with having all the keys and all the open
doors of the Universe.

When you open your eyes and come back out of your deep
meditation cloud, you gently have a vision and realize that
Spirit has guided me to place you at the door, and you are
now the greeter, showing others their very own
Universe within.

Learning love is our daily practice.

Pull Yourself Closer to Your Heart

When you feel something pulling on your heart, it's probably God and the Universe pulling on you to align you with the power of your heart and not the desires of the world, which you may think it is.

Sex, money, food — all natural for you to want and crave, but go beyond that. Go beyond, into the superb and supreme consciousness of your heart and the Universe's love, the Angels' love, and feel that bliss.

Go beyond the body, beyond the mind, and blossom and sail blissfully into the depths of your heart in meditation. Wake up into your Angelic conscious heart more and more, and learn to do it more and more. With your meditation practice, you will feel better and better, shedding more and more of your ego and seeing your own projects and the actions you are making to create your reality in a way of good.

Take yourself from the world and go to your room and meditate. Meditate. Meditate. Through silent meditation, you will learn what it is to feel the presence of God. We are not the body or the mind. We are the pulling and pulsing light of the soul. Beyond the desire of experience, in a matter made up of molecules and form, in our thoughts or ideas, we are the vibration of Spirit that is calling our energy to stay fully one in that love, and opening more, activating more in the light circuitry, light energy.

We are light energy. We are love. We choose eternity and see the other side is destruction of self. The self listens to the calling and deepest desire and highest love of the heart to become One with the higher self, the Angels, and God-current. It is beyond words to describe a thing, self is what you think you are. The higher self is God and the Angels.

Wine & Dine

You wine and dine with all your friends, so why can't you
dine so deeply with God in silent sitting meditation?

Give the Creator some love too!

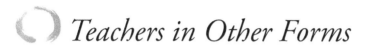 *Teachers in Other Forms*

Not every Spiritual teacher or master sits around in a loincloth with their students. I know beings that can do things and perform healings and miraculous things that also wear normal clothes. They don't publish books and are not even in the public eye. There are some real Undercover Yogis.

Spirit runs deep through all souls and goes far beyond media, what you hear, or what you see.

Once you fully have the desire to know God you see him/ her/ it/ everywhere working in all things big or small.

Spreading Divine Energy

Some months, it's better to stay inside and meditate
for hours and hours every day

than to be outside for years and never learn to send
light to our friends, family, and all beings

while strengthening our hearts and minds so our practical, mental
minds can tap more into our hearts and spread that charged
energy to everyone we come in contact with.

Yoga Stretches & Silent Meditation

Many people do yoga stretches, work out, or listen to music to be strong or be in a relaxing space, body, mind, and soul. But I also encourage you to do more silent meditation and cleanse your body, too. Silent meditation and a clean body is where the beauty begins.

You have never experienced anything close to true bliss or the true joy and knowing of God if you haven't experienced lots of silent meditation with a clean body.

Practice silent meditation ceaselessly. Stop watching movies and TV all the time. Take breaks from those TVs—a little bit is all right, but pull yourself away from the radio and TVs.

Give you heart and soul to the Creator and you will know true happiness and feel Divinely blessed.

Please, I encourage you; you will feel so much better. You must meditate, meditate, and then meditate some more.

Someone Asked Me a Simple Question

What does your heart yearn for?

I thought about it a little, and then I answered simply.

It yearns for all beings to love all beings infinitely. It yearns for everything true, good, and beautiful. It yearns to always remember everything in my experiences as so. It yearns for peace in the village of our whole world. It yearns to fully experience and express my gratitude for the Universe's love that I have been so blessed to experience. It yearns for nothing, because I already have everything that I could have ever dreamed of.

Daily I sit, speechlessly in awe, enjoying my still, silent meditation practice to show my gratitude for the Divine, all the Angels, and the Universe, and to help my heart to always remind my mind to always remember the beautiful, mystical, potently magical miracles of life.

 *Oneness*

Meditate! Dwell in God, dwell in God!

He who is devoted fully to be more in Divine communion and Christ consciousness will do or give up anything asked of a Master in a split second to reach that absolute attainment.

This is just a metaphor, but you know what I mean. :)

In our human lives, we know deep within us that we are more valuable and more capable than what the illusions or the ignorant are telling us.

Go deep within and devote your heart to the Creator.

Lift your Spirits to know the ever-knowable joys that will come with your devotion to self-realization, and through your daily meditations, journey to supreme oneness with all things.

Gratitude and Gravity

Keep moving forward to what kind of life you want to live. Give time to get perspective on what you feel matters, keeping the planet and the people in mind. True fulfillment in the heart comes from self-love and love for God; the others in the middle will sway from that. Self-love and love for life and the Creator are the best things in the world; everything else is temporary. No matter the money you make or how hard you physically work, your heart will want true peace and comfort. Expanding the love in the heart is powerful. Love is the doorway and the key.

Persevering, giving heart, loving mind, cleansing the body, eating healthy, discerning who influences you, healing work, exercising, nature, silent meditation, meditation, meditation.

Divine Strength

All my strength comes from pain and compassion. Beyond that is the great light of Spirit, Divine Love, God. We all fill the reservoir of our hearts as much as we can to live and to love daily. Many little obstacles in the dream world of reality seem to chip away some of our energy. The unbending courage of the heart to remain open, gentle, and strong is our greatest gift. In this balance, we surrender at the feet of the Divine Mother and Father, the Angels, the Universe; that is what guides our way home. And here is where the diamonds of the heart lay as shining specks of stardust.

All walk down the magical carpet in life hoping to be ready to fly home, to transition and feel ready for a good departure. Angelic forces transport us with undeniably super-expanded love and with the wisdom and knowing of the challenges we face here on Earth. You are born with the mothers, fathers, sisters, and brothers of God. Many of us have played different roles for each other in different lives. You are never alone, and you are Divinely loved always!

Love is all there is and is all that is of value. Remember, you are loved and are never alone.

Soul Journey

My heart has been through thousands of wars, and
only a meditative master of love can spear it.

Many have a chance to get close to my heart, for the entrance
is at eternity's door and is for those who sense, see, touch, and
taste its presence. I dance in the mystery of meditation, I sail
deeply on the backs of miracles and oracles where Angels set
their wings and prayed, in times long ago, when there were
no people, no water, no land . . . just God!

When and where the Angels knelt down to their own illuminated
feet in the canvas of creation, on a place, a palace, a temple of
light called Paradise, trillions of Angelic beings roam creation
with their hearts wide open, opening up more hearts on their
way all around the galaxies, all the way to the Spirit circuits of
the Universe, on to the superhighway, to the inhabited planets
designed and designated for them and for their mission to
uplift all mortals with the indwelling Spirit. The light
and love of all. The love of love. The love of God.

Our Heavenly Choice— Body Cleansing!

At points in our lives, we may feel a little low in energy, weighed down negative perceptions. We may think they have great power over us or that somehow they have been instilled in us by the confusions of others or ourselves. But this negativity is not you, you see! In the world there is, naturally, negativity and positivity!

It is in the natural fabric of the Universe! Too much negativity can be of great harm to ourselves or others, and positivity will always be of great benefit for all beings! Sometimes we may just simply need to do some liver cleansing and detoxify our bodies to get rid of built-up cholesterol and toxins that can stay in the liver and get released into the bloodstream, making us feel low energy, creating negative thought patterns, and making us feel depressed.

Let us clear this mental slavery and body pain and find the loving keys to positivity within us, whatever that is that we need to do, and arrive to our great success. Our perceptions are our own choice. Our will to do the inner and outer work is our own choice. We have the power within us to live in the golden estate of heaven on Earth, finding all the love overflowing within our own hearts, in the blissful realms of the Angels and God.

I believe in you!

Your own special, mystical, magical, blissful heaven awaits you!

Cleanse the body. Eat healthy. Exercise. Do yoga. Meditate!

More Love Beyond Your Imagination

Now I must ask:

What if almost everything you desire from this
world is a lie traceable by heaven?

What if there is something more?
Would you be open to it?

I already know your answer, and yes, it is true. God is infinite.

Isn't it so unimaginably incomprehensible that you would
not try to comprehend the vastness of it all?

Wow, the Universe is so VAST!

V_ery
A_mazing
S_ublime
T_ime

The Time is Now

Doorway through Pain

The extreme pain we go through can work as a great benefit to us, believe it or not. I know, because I have experienced much of it. For when we want to truly feel better, if we choose to heal and have that deep desire, we will find our way. The Universe will open doors to us; we have to choose to walk through the doors that we feel are right for them. Hopefully, on the other side of the doors we choose, our extreme pain will be finally and fully gone, or manageable, by our effort to walk through the door. Then we get to experience being so grateful for our new life of gratitude and our very own paradise within.

The Time is Now

Meditate because you can. If there is time, then there is always time to meditate. Expansion of the heart into the understanding of love, yourself, and the Universe is necessary. The time is always now. Go deep into it.

Heart Love

The heart stretches and grows immensely. Breaking and shattering open can also allow for deeper growth to occur.

Sure, deep heartbreak doesn't always need to happen; the heart can go without it. But when it does happen, we can let the shattering of the heart open us up to so much depth in our own individual healing. We can feel the body, the soul, feel all the gems and diamonds of the heart pour out, releasing that energy more and more, giving and receiving love even deeper, building up even more desire to share what we learned to help others. You see?

It's hard at times, but pain is still useful to guide us to feel even better than we did before and choose manifestations closer to our true desires, our highest, deepest mature desires.

The oceans are all salt water like our tears, and just look at all the life and beauty that lives happily in the ocean. So much good comes out of letting ourselves open. At some point, we will want to say to the Universe, "Give me your best shot!" out of our brave devotion. We may also want to say, "I am ready for anything! I will stay devoted to the Divine no matter what is going on, still keeping my practice, doing the inner work, doing my daily meditations and other things that help me feel better. Gaining more experience, staying in gratitude, knowing I am loved, enhancing my Angelic vision to be clearer to make the best and highest decisions for all."

We are all learning how to open, learning who to open to, learning how to let Spirit open us. We learn to be discerning, open, aware, gaining more wisdom with our hearts. People can hurt our hearts, but we can still learn to keep our hearts open for the world. Spirit always has our back. Spirit gives us exactly what we need. We grow, we grow, we grow… and then we grow some more.

Pure Devotion

Bathing in meditation with clearness and clarity in the mind, we feel the fullness of God deep within our hearts.

The Angels, fairies, all the great teachers of light, all the light beings, all the stars in the sky, all things made in the physical reality, are here waiting for everyone to realize how loved they are and how much love exists within each heart.

Infinite potential. The magnificent love is within you. The love is who you are. Open your eyes and wake up.

Expressions of Divine Love

Writing is my tool. It is how I show the open lovers of life and the ones having a little Earthly troubles that God exists and the Universe has a voice, just like your little body and your little throbbing heart.

Knowing the existence of love and that God is real and fully present in your body, your soul, and your life is the greatest gift. It is one of the biggest beginnings and realizations gifted to you for your future great realizations in your Earthly and universal carrier. May you learn and know that all of your desires are yearning for you to know this. The soul wants true substance. The soul wants the greatest love for you.

May you thirst for this great light before you, and may you feel and know this peace.

Even if you comune with God in a temple or a church, may you not *need* them to *find* this, but only by and through the golden temple within your own heart, which has been polished by your own love, and by the Divine Universe, which is shining great showers of light over you by the trillions of Angels and stars, destined to keep beaming over the world for centuries and centuries to come.

God pervades all space, all time, all things, and through all limitations of the mind.

Universe—God

I want to feel all of your love wrapped around
me like a warm Angelic blanket.

I want to be forever at your sleepover,

and we could meditate ourselves to sleep every night.

The Love Within

Working on yourself through cleansing your liver, exercising, eating healthy, being around other good influences, doing yoga, and sitting in silent meditation will bring you more inner peace, more understanding, more contentment, more happiness and joy, naturally. Be easy on yourself; take it slowly, but still do your good work and you will see the fruits and the benefits of your forward movement to where you want to be, and to be in peace for where you are now.

You are loved dearly, and your heart's desire will lead you. You will find others who are more advanced, who will give you more strength, give you a little boost, a little push to help you fly. The more you find love within your heart, the more you will give it back to the world naturally through just your simple presence.

Yes, some may judge you, without a clear perspective, for any of the little innocent mistakes you have made, even if you are way past these mistakes and now make better or the highest decisions. They judge by their own default, not seeing who you truly are. But you and your family and your good friends and your Angels know your heart of hearts and where your ever-growing, expansive, expanding love and highest potential sit.

Yes, some people can be mean, but that is like a little drop of dirt in a big, beautiful, snowy meadow compared to all the loving people in the world. There will always be many who see the good you do and the light you share in the world.

May you stay strong in your path of good. May the Angels give you strength. May you always remember the great love of the Universe and not let others' little negativity or misjudgments affect you too much, for you know your heart, and you know your path.

Send your love and light to all beings, even those who throw their stones and judgments.

Have empathy for them, for if you know who you are and you are walking in the world in a good way, then it is inevitable that the little pebbles they throw will come back and hit them on the cosmic wheel. Keep your gratitude for life, your grateful heart for love, and the expanding, growing gratitude for your own love, which is for yourself, your family, your friends, and all beings.

Divine Love Always

I hope everything you truly desire is revealed to you and embraced and is made manifest for all you are and do in the world, being of a Mother, a Father and a university of Angels.

Divine Love always! All beings, yogis and yoginis.
Blessings always.

Little Bites

If you bite into a sour apple, you can't blame or get mad at the tree or God or life. Growth lies through the discernment, awareness, experience, and study of whether the apple is ripe.

Is it good? Does it nurture you? Bring you energy? Help you be in balance? Sustain your heart? Energize your blood? Restore your system? Enliven your cells?

It takes time and discernment and a clearness of wisdom from experience and intuition to see things for what they are. Expanding heart, expanding perception, expanding intuition, expanding love.

Nibble slowly to make sure that what you think you really want is really for your highest and best. We are all learning.

244   *The Treasures of Divine Love*

The Treasures of Divine Love

Love to you, Divine, loving, mystical, magical, translucent, open, aware, universal, galactivated, supernal, sweet, intelligent, auricly-stimulating treasure of Divine Angelic love.

Eternal Prayer Flags

Prayers and peace will forever flow through the existence of time. Divine Love has no limits. The Universe breeds masters and individuals growing ever more present in the presence of itself, the Angels, the higher self, the Angelic perspective, God.

For those not yet praying, and for those not yet practicing deep silent meditation: You are loved dearly beyond your thoughts and perceptions. Your soul and Spirit know a deep love beyond the body. The many practicing loving beings who are dedicated to ceaselessly working on themselves are praying, sending you love and light, and waiting to see you in your deepest love, embracing you, open, strong, gentle, and compassionate always, wanting and patiently waiting to welcome you home.

Go Beyond

Go beyond your belief or thought that the Universe's love—God's love—*might* be real, and know it *is* real! You must first desire to know. Your strong thirst for sure knowing will eventually find you and you will forever know that truth. You will never question the magnitude of the Divine magnificence again. You will see in time and experience what calm feelings it will give to you.

First, you will experience your feelings of love for life. Then, seeing the spark of God in the shimmers of light in others' eyes, then your desire to know God will reveal that God exists undoubtedly. Then, eventually, you will hear, feel, see the clear communication.

Eat healthy, cleanse, do yoga, exercise, sit in silent meditation, rest, swim, dance, play. Keep your heart open. Love.

A Divine Love Story

This love story is way more than about you. It is the magical
stew, the Divine glue. It is the rainbow, auric, Angelic, elegant,
Spiritualized alphabet, glimmering through its own raindrop-
Spirited value molecules, draped by its very own golden globe temple
polished horoscopes, granted "Grammy" nominations
and "Oscars" through and for its own Divine presence.

This Divine, loving, universal university of cosmic bliss waves,
calculated and constructed, can't even be properly translated into
proper English at times, because in its own Divine storytelling,
there exist moments that surpass understanding of thought, and
the Creator of the Universe transcends and supervenes all things,
pervades all space and time. The meditated creator who gathers
bits of the master's wisdom and knowing in meditation, with the
feelings that overshadow and overshine the far more wisdomatic
thought-forms even beyond thought, determinedly and undoubtedly
magnetizes more love increasingly, and so indeed!

To actually articulate this storytelling story from a living, expressed
maker of light through the vessel of the upholding Spirit holder is to
suggest that the new created story to be revealed is by you and your
own devotion to love.

So now you get it, right? It is your turn!

Make this story what every storyteller wishes to tell,
and send love and light to all, like Tinkerbell.

You Want Inner Peace?

You want happiness? You want to be a super yogi or yogini?

You want to understand why you are here, how
you got here, and where you are going?

You can do all the yoga and stretching as much as you want. You
can stretch the best or hold the best pose. You can physically be
in prime shape, but if you are not going deep into your heart
and doing the inner work and learning silent sitting meditation,
then you are missing the point of it all. If you want to shift for
the better and more greatly benefit your life, then you must learn
silent sitting meditation, too. You can eat healthy, cleanse the
liver, exercise, but you must learn silent sitting meditation, too!

Come on! I know you can do it! If everyone really knew the
extreme benefits of silent sitting meditation, then every
person in the world would do it!

Go deep in this path. Just nibbling little prayers won't do.

You've got this.

I believe in you—little efforts every day.

Awaken through Imagination

So many memories of beautiful rainbows
shining over the mountains and down on the big green trees,
songs and whisperings of the Divine melodies, while the people
sit planting seeds in the rain,
giggling the raindrops in as they fall directly down on my
forehead and onto my third eye.

An ocean of life glimmers through these feelings that I get from
this wet, awakened dream,
beaming colors while the great mermaids eat jelly beans through
the thoughts and hopes of butterflies playing with fairies in a
meadow of compassion,
sharing tea and giving thanks,
sharing tea and giving thanks,
sharing tea and giving thanks,
like there was nothing else to do.

Giving thanks for all the Angels' wings landing down on all
of heaven's miracles, sending love and light to all beings with a
laughter streaming from the Divine Love that showers the calm
rivers of stardust and warm, silent meditation,

I fall asleep as I awake again, only to fall asleep and awake again,
and sit up in a yoga pose, illuminating a golden light in the
green lusciousness of the jungle forest, on the back of a magical
elephant who is breathing in my thoughts, in and out, and is
slowly turning his gaze to look at me as I start waking up from
this dream.

One of the biggeset strengths is in knowing that we are loved.

It's All Love.

Love and Support

I have experienced a profound amount of love from other Spirit brothers and sisters on this planet. It is very nice to know that there are such amazingly loving, caring, compassionate, sweet, empathetic, kind, loyal, brave, courageous, passionate, open-hearted people who are amazingly miraculous in my eyes.

There are so many beings, humans, souls, and such large numbers of us who are here to support, care, share, help, and relate to one another.

This here is something we all are a part of, and we should be grateful, amazed, surprised, and blown away by our togetherness as a human family, to go forward and expand more in this understanding of peace, compassion, empathy, and support for our expansion as evolving human beings. This understanding can teach us all to not be so hard on ourselves, especially when we are trying our best to move forward in love, in the understanding of ourselves and how we got here, what we are doing here, and where we are going.

We all can realize our divinity and strength. We all can be bright and loving naturally. We have all come through rough times here on this planet, together for thousands of years. We still have lots of work to do. We all could be more opened, centered, caring, helpful, and understanding with one another, although we have large amounts of confusion of how we got here, what we are doing here, and where we are going. We all have done well considering our situation here on this rock–planet–vessel–spaceship, flying through space at millions of miles an hour.

It is logical to think that we have done okay, considering our circumstances here on this planet, with our slowly evolving awareness of how we got here, what we are doing here, and where we are going. Some people still think we are the remnants of a big explosion, "THE BIG BANG." Do we look like the remnants of a big explosion to you? I think we are pretty put together, well designed, thought out, created, engineered in a way, and well-organized organisms of life, don't you? We are amazing miracles, God dust, and the more we realize this fact, the more we will strengthen powerfully as one big family in unity. Meditation brings us closer to our higher wisdom, and eventually, we are fully fused and one with it.

Let Love Rain Down All Over

I was thinking what if no one enjoyed what I write, would I still write. It's something I have probably pondered before. It took some time to think about it again, maybe a few seconds, and I realized that of course I would. I started writing before I ever showed anyone. It was for me, God, the world as well but it was for me my heart, it was my own expressions and God first. My love for myself, my family and God gave me more compassion for the world, and that gave me courage to share with the world. The world also fueled my fire for The Divine, and I saw great need of inspiration for myself and others. My writings came after thousands of hours of silent sitting meditation and then it just started to flow out almost naturally like I had always done it. But I didn't always do it. My life growing up was full of sadness, pain, and fear, and I fought to stay alive. My family and others helped me to strive on and think about the life I could have someday, and they reminded me of how nice of a person I was and how I had so much potential.

My pain, fear and sadness was severe and many times I lost hope. I prayed, got angry, thought hard, worked hard, didn't work at all, did whatever I could to build more strength and positivity to see why life was worth living, and yet it still didn't work. I met a lady who channeled the Angels, and I finally heard the Angels speak to me clearly in my ear. I finally knew what I always wanted to know. I knew that God really does exist, the Angels do exist, and there is a greater love and compassion beyond what we sometimes feel: A love that loves us so much and is wishing our highest and best. Something is always there reaching out to us and hoping we learn to feel its presence as much as we can. I figured out that I love to love, love to connect with other sweet souls and share this truth, this magic, this awakening, this love, this awareness. I want to share this gift as much as I can before I leave this world, and my intention is to make a good change in the world towards world peace.

Our intentions are very powerful.

Spirit to Spirit

I wish for my children to one day look up to me and say, "Dad, how did you write the most amazing, beautiful pearls for the world?" And I will look at them and say, "I was created by the Spirit, my mind, body, and soul. I was given all my experiences by the Spirit. Spirit led me further to Spirit, and so, throughout my life, I sailed deep within in meditation to express the deep valleys and pathways of my heart and my connection to Spirit. So, with all that, I would have to say that God is how I wrote at all."

"How do you know God really exists, Dad?"

I will laugh and say,

"Look all around you, dear ones. How could there not be a master maker that has created us all, all the souls of the world? Everything is showing you God's existence. The animals, the trees, the planets throughout all the galaxies. Billions and billions of galaxies within one Universe, and there are trillions and trillions. Look at what miracles we are. How amazing to be alive at all and to have the breath of life. How grateful to have all the senses to experience any of this. How special to feel this love at all for ourselves, family, friends, all beings. The deep love within the heart: that is a special gift. All the love within your heart is for you. It is for you to feel. Your heart will expand so much throughout your whole life that sometimes it will even hurt with growing pains, just like your little teeth did. Through your breath and meditation, the love in your heart will be so full that you will constantly be in awe and wonder, and what gems and pearls you will find on your journey! In allowing and opening yourself to the Spirit through your desire and intentions, you will also see that the waves of love will forever be opening your heart more and more, gently crashing on the sands of your inner peace, right to your feet. I also know the higher self, the Spirit, the Creator, the Universe — God — exists because I am very blessed to have clear communication with all of it."

Then I will laugh and say, "Read my books again, silly. What do you mean, how do I know if God exists?"

Within You

Look within for your light.

Ask the Angels and guides to be with you.

Tell them that you are humbled to work with them.

The next pages of your life are for you.

Your turn.

Notes for your own thoughts, affirmations, or quotes.

258 🪷 *The Treasures of Divine Love*

Made in the USA
Middletown, DE
26 October 2022